Hinduism for Our Times

HINDUISM FOR OUR TIMES

Arvind Sharma

DELHI
OXFORD UNIVERSITY PRESS
BOMBAY CALCUTTA MADRAS
1996

Oxford University Press, Walton Street, Oxford OX2 6DP
Oxford New York
Athens Aukland Bangkok Bombay
Calcutta Cape Town Dar Es Salaam Delhi
Florence Hong Kong Istanbul Karachi
Kuala Lampur Madras Madrid Melbourne
Mexico City Nairobi Paris Singapore
Taipei Tokyo Toronto
and associates in
Berlin Ibadan

ISBN 0 19 563749 6

Hinduism

Typeset at All India Press, Pondicherry 605001
Printed at Saurabh Print-O-Pack, Noida
and published by Neil O'Brien, Oxford University Press
YMCA Library Building, Jai Singh Road, New Delhi 110001

The material of this book was originally delivered as a series of lectures on 7, 9, 11, 13 and 15 December 1993, at the Max Mueller Bhavan, New Delhi.

For
Georg, An-Rye and Marie
in friendship

Contents

Chapter 1

Contemporary Hinduism: Its Sources and Resources

I

In addressing the question of Hinduism for our times we may begin by asking: Is Hinduism supposed to keep up with the times or are the times supposed to keep up with Hinduism? Both strands of thought equally constitute the basis of our contemporary faith. The passage with which Professor S. Radhakrishnan concludes his slim volume, *The Hindu View of Life*, which though slim in size speaks volumes as it were, could well serve as our starting point, for it enshrines the view that Hinduism must keep up with the times. He concludes with eloquent simplicity:

> After a long winter of some centuries, we are today in one of the creative periods of Hinduism. We are beginning to look upon our ancient faith with fresh eyes. We feel that our society is in a condition of unstable equilibrium. There is much wood that is dead and diseased that has to be cleared away. Leaders of Hindu thought and practice are convinced that the times require, not a surrender of the basic principles of Hinduism, but a restatement of them with special reference to the needs of a more complex and mobile social order. Such an attempt will only be the repetition of a process which has occurred a number of times in the history of Hinduism. The work of readjustment is in process. Growth is slow when roots are deep. But those who light a little candle in the darkness will help to make the whole sky aflame.[1]

These views were expressed in 1926 as he concluded the Upton lectures, delivered at Manchester College, Oxford and are still held by many in 1995; that unless Hinduism changes with the times, it will be relegated to the status of a permanent delinquent in the race of modernity. One may now put alongside it another perspective which would rather that the world were moulded in the shape of Hinduism, than that Hinduism was moulded in the shape of the world. Flashes of this perspective are found even in Radhakrishnan, as when he writes: 'To obliterate every other religion than one's own is a sort of bolshevism in religion which we must try to prevent. We can do so only if we accept something like the Hindu solution...'[2] But a full-throated assertion of this view is found in the speeches of Swami Vivekananda, in his famous exhortation to the young men of Madras to cast the world in the image of Hinduism:

> Where are the men ready to go out to every country in the world with the messages of the great sages of India? Where are the men who are ready to sacrifice everything, so that this message shall reach every corner of the world? Such heroic souls are wanted to help the spread of truth... We must go out, we must conquer the world through our spirituality and philosophy. There is no other alternative, we must do it or die. The only condition of national life, of awakened and vigorous national life, is the conquest of the world by Indian thought.[3]

Vivekananda appeals not to Hinduism but to Indian spirituality of which Hindu spirituality is a part, but only a part and we can't confuse the part with the whole—arrogate to Hindu spirituality the status of Indian spirituality. Even when he appeals to a specifically Hindu element, the Vedānta, we must again avoid the same pitfall of identifying Vedānta with Hinduism, as of identifying Hindu with Indian spirituality. Let me then turn to a less porous statement on this point. It is, surprisingly, offered by Mahatma Gandhi, who provides two unequivocal statements, so it seems to me, of the point I am trying to make.

The first of these pertains to proselytization. Mahatma Gandhi told C. F. Andrews:

> If a person wants to believe in the Bible let him say so, but why should he discard his own religion? This proselytization will mean no peace in the

world. Religion is a very personal matter. We should by living the life according to our lights share the best with one another, thus adding to the sum total of human effort to reach God.[4]

Correctly or incorrectly Mahatma Gandhi believed that the absence of such proselytization was the hallmark of Hinduism, for he declared, 'In my opinion there is no such thing as proselytism in Hinduism...',[5] consistently with his famous pronouncement:

So, we can only pray, if we are Hindus, not that a Christian should become a Hindu; or if we are Mussalmans, not that a Hindu, or a Christian should become a Mussalman; nor should we even secretly pray that anyone should be converted; but our inmost prayer should be that a Hindu should be a better Hindu, a Muslim a better Muslim, and a Christian a better Christian. That is the fundamental truth of fellowship.[6]

T.M.P. Mahadevan felicitously distinguishes between vertical conversion: 'From lower to the higher conception of God' and horizontal conversion merely 'from one formal faith to another'.[7]

But one might ask: Are all religions equally good? Sir Francis Younghusband responded in the Gandhian spirit by asking the counter-question: 'Are all mothers equally good?'[8] Kakasaheb Kalelkar brought out the full implication of this simile when he explained:

Indeed every one of us regards his own mother as the best, but does he, therefore, expect or ask others to give up their own mothers and adopt his own? In other words, just as one's own mother is *best for oneself*, so is every one's religion the best, each for himself; just as one's own country is *best for oneself*, every one's religion is best, each for himself. The equality of all religions lies in each being adequate or best for its respective adherents.[9]

I have dwelt on this maternal metaphor at some length for I discovered, quite by accident, that when other religions try to adopt this Gandhian position they find themselves inadvertently using the same metaphor. For instance, Professor Krister Stendahl concluded his lecture, delivered on 27 February 1992 at the Center for the Study of World Religions at Harvard University as follows:

Now my final point is this. It is a well-known one and I don't know why it has dawned on me so slowly. I have referred to texts. These are *our* texts. Each minority has its texts; what its history has recorded, what God has recorded in the hearts of the people. Their writing is shaped by their experiences.

These are out texts. Out of our perspectives we interpret them. When a child is born—I guess women can talk better about this—but I would guess that the child's, the baby's, world does not consist of much more than itself and the mother's breast. That's the whole world and one of the things that happens as we grow up is that it dawns upon us that other children have sucked other breasts. The process of sorting out such facts is called maturation. That's what maturation is.[10]

I would like to draw your attention back to the initial insight in the passage and the language in which it is expressed: '... one of the things that happens as we grow up is that it dawns upon us that other children have sucked at other breasts. The process of sorting out such facts is called maturation. That's what maturation is.'[11]

So one way in which Gandhi would that the world was shaped by Hinduism is the attitude towards proselytization or religious conversion and the other, the second one is the doctrine of *varṇa*, which has nothing to do with caste so far as Mahatma Gandhi was concerned. Mahatma Gandhi writes:

Though the law of *varna* is a special discovery of some Hindu seer, it has universal application. Every religion has some distinguishing characteristic, but if it expresses a principle or law, it ought to have universal application. That is how I look at the law of *varna*. The world may ignore it today but it will have to accept it in the time to come.[12]

Elsewhere he states even more explicitly:

The Hindu civilization has survived the Egyptian, the Assyrian and the Babylonian. The Christian is but two thousand years old. The Islamic is but of yesterday. Great as both these are they are still in my humble opinion in the making. Christian Europe is not at all Christian, but is groping, and so in my opinion is Islam still groping for its great secret, and there is today a competition, healthy as also extremely unhealthy and ugly, between these three great religions.

As years go by, the conviction is daily growing upon me that *varna* is the law of man's being and therefore as necessary for Christianity and Islam, as it has been necessary for Hinduism and has been its saving.[13]

II

However, whether we hold the view that the world is going to change Hinduism or the view that Hinduism is going to change the world or that each is going to change the other in a manner not known to either of them or to any of us yet, our discussion must remain anchored in the truism that times change—whether we change them or they change us. At the moment I am not inclined to take sides on this issue but rather to look at both sides of the picture. The present represents the perennial interface of the past and the future: of times gone by and the times to be, or, to alter the metaphor, in this great traffic in time between the past and the future, are we, who are in the present, just bystanders? Or are we more but not much more: Just passing through? Or are we such more? Are we not engaged in a process of constant negotiation between the two? Are we not receiving impressions from the past as well as giving shape to the future? If we are being circumscribed by the givenness of the past then are we not, at the same time, being invited into the open circumference of the future? After all, a tradition can never be transferred, it can only be transmitted and its transmission is a running dialogue between change and continuity. We are where we are and we do not know whether we are at the cutting edge or at the periphery. We may never know; perhaps history will, but as history is a record of the past as read through the lens of the present, it can change its mind too. However, the precariousness of the present does not compromise its seriousness. It may be nebulous but we must not be disingenuous; we must revert to the question of Hinduism for our times: whether it is changed by the times or whether it changes the times or whether the two interact not merely mechanically but also reciprocally.

I would like to begin then by focusing on the question of changes wrought in Hinduism and defer, in the interest of clarity, for subsequent discussion, the question of changes that could be wrought by Hinduism. How does, in other words, Hinduism handle change?

III

For a tradition which describes itself as *sanātana dharma*, the question is not an easy one to answer. We are told that when Jesus told Pilate: I preach the truth, Pilate said (almost in jest) What is truth? (John 18:38–39) and did not wait for an answer. But if Jesus were a Hindu he could have told him that truth is eternal and Pilate could have waited as long as he liked. There is, after all, no lost time in eternity.

The word *sanātana* is sometimes translated as eternal, and for a tradition which also calls itself *vaidika* the philosophical temptation to do so can be overwhelming, given the putative eternality of the Vedas. Nor is such an interpretation entirely misplaced. The word Hinduism after all is not a Hindu word. It has been pointed out that:

> The indigenous names by which Hinduism is known are *sanātana-dharma* and *vaidika-dharma*. *Sanātana-dharma* means eternal religion and is expressive of the truth that religion as such knows no age. It is coeval with life. It is the food of the spirit in man. The other name, *vaidika-dharma*, means the religion of the Vedas. The Vedas are the foundational Scriptures of the Hindus; and... they imply not merely the four Vedas, *Rg*, *Yajur*, *Sāma*, and *Atharva*, but all words that speak of God. 'Veda' is a significant name, meaning God-knowledge or God-science. Hinduism regards as its authority the religious experience of the ancient sages of India. It does not owe its origin to any historical personage or prophet. Buddhism, Christianity and Islam are founded religions. Their dates are definite, since their authors are known. No such date or founder can be cited as marking the beginning of Hinduism. Hence it is called *sanātana* and *vaidika*, ancient and revealed.[14]

In this passage one detects a semantic shift in the meaning attached to the word sanātana. First it is translated as eternal but after the Vedas have been alluded to, the same word is translated towards the end not as 'eternal' but as 'ancient', once the sages have been brought into the picture. The word sanātana can mean eternal. This is true, but it is not the whole truth. Something can be wholly true and yet not true of the whole. As P.V. Kane explains at some length, from another perspective:

> the words 'sanātana dharma' do not mean that Dharma always stands still or is immutable; all that those words means is that our culture is very ancient

and has a long tradition behind it but they do not mean that Dharma permits no change. As a matter of fact fundamental changes in conceptions, beliefs and practices have been made from ancient times to the medieval times by means of various devices.[15]

P.V. Kane draws attention to a few of these. At one time the entire corpus of the Vedas was uniformly sacred but the *Muṇḍaka Upaniṣad* (I.I.5) designates the four Vedas as inferior knowledge (*aparā vidyā*) and the knowledge of the immutable *brahmin* as the higher *vidyā*. Similarly, in the *Chāndogya Upaniṣad* (VII.1.4) the four Vedas and several other branches of knowledge are called by Sanatkumāra (whom Nārada approached for instruction) mere name (*nāma*). Yajñas were the most important religious practice in the early Vedic period, but the *Muṇḍaka Upaniṣad* (I.2.7) designates them as leaky boats and regards those who hold them as the best thing to be fools. Students of Hinduism are well aware of the changes that have occurred in views regarding 'anuloma marriages, on the topic of whose food may be partaken even by a brāhmaṇa, the abrogation of many Vedic practices by the doctrine of Kalivarjya (matters forbidden in Kali age) &c.' Many Hindu legal texts and even extralegal texts:

> expressly provide that one should not observe but give up what was once dharma, if it has come to be hateful to the people and if it would end in unhappiness... The Śantiparva expressly states that what was *adharma* (in one age) may become dharma in another and that dharma and adharma are both subject to the limitations of country and time.[16]

In accordance with these views Hinduism is like the sky: It is eternal and yet it is changing all the time, a witness to the alternation of day and night. Or to follow up with a nocturnal metaphor: It is like the firmament which appears fixed but is changing all the time, which changes all the time but appears fixed.

IV

No amount of metaphorical jugglery can, however, conceal the fact that Hinduism changes, and that it changes with the times. The question is: How does it do so? For although the dharma is not fixed its sources seem to be; although the firmament is not fixed the four cardinal points are. These cardinal points, the sources of dharma, according to one verse in Manu (II.6.12) are: (1) *śruti* or the Vedas; (2) *smṛti* or sacred tradition; (3) *sadācāra* or the customs of virtuous men and (4) *ātmatuṣṭi*: what is congenial to oneself, or perhaps to the 'conscience'.

Now it seems to me that at least three understandings of these four sources of dharma can be identified with Hinduism. These might be described as pyramidal, percolative or kaleidoscopic, depending on whether the four sources are viewed from top downwards; from bottom upwards; or independently on their own. According to the hierarchical understanding of the four sources, the Vedas are the first source and 'self-satisfaction' is the last, and one takes recourse to the later sources only when the earlier ones offer no guidance. This seems to correspond to Manu's understanding as interpreted by Bühler.[17]

Mahatma Gandhi, on the other hand, virtually reversed the order. About the Vedas he declared: 'I am not going to burn a spotless horse because the *Vedas* are reported to have advised, tolerated or sanctioned the sacrifice.'[18] As for the custodians of the Vedas, the Brahmins, he said:

> Mere knowledge of the *Vedas* cannot make our *brahmanas* spiritual preceptors. If it did, Max Muller would have become one. The *brahmana* who has understood the religion of today will certainly give *Vedic* learning a secondary place and propagate the religion of the spinning wheel, relieve the hunger of the millions of his starving countrymen and only then, and not until then, lose himself in *Vedic* studies.[19]

In relation to the smṛtis he wanted 'some authoritative body that would revise all that passes under the name of scriptures [*smṛtis*], expurgate all the texts that have no moral value or are contrary to the fundamentals of religion and morality, and present such an edition for the guidance of the Hindus'.[20] It was much more important for Gandhi that we 'ponder over the lives and examples of Harishchandra, Prahlad, Ramachandra, Imam Hasan and Imam Hussain, the Christian saints, etc.' This, it seems, would have constituted *sadācāra* for him while, of course, the pride of place was accorded to the Inner Voice.

Viewed in this light Mahatma Gandhi inverted the hierarchy of the sources of dharma and brought about cardinal changes in Hinduism by making ordinal changes within it.

I referred earlier to the inner voice. It seems that Mahatma Gandhi may have heard and heeded such a voice even at the tender age of twelve:

It was a time when he was beginning to think seriously about morality and codes of conduct. He was twelve, in his second year at the high school, when he began to question the accepted codes of the Indian caste system. A scavenger called Uka, who belonged to the lowest caste, was employed in the house to clean out the latrines. If anyone of a superior caste accidentally touched the scavenger, then he must at once purify himself by performing his ablutions. Mohandas had a great fondness for Uka and could see no reason why he should be regarded as an inferior. Very respectfully he suggested to his parents that they were wrong to regard the scavenger in this way; an accidental touch could not be a sin and Uka was a man like other men. His mother reminded him that it was not necessary to perform one's ablutions after touching a scavenger; instead, one could touch a Muslim, thus transferring the pollution to someone who was free of the taboos of the Hindu religion.[21]

A third consideration must also now be introduced: That in effect, each source of dharma in some way or another can enjoy an elevated rank in a display of juridical kathenotheism. The supremacy of the Vedas has been alluded to. The problem arose at the end of the period of Vedic revelation: Who will guide us now that revelation may have ceased? Allama Iqbal interpreted the end of verbal prophecy within Islam as indicating that henceforth human beings had to rely on their own resources for guidance,[22] a position uncannily anticipated by Yāska in perhaps the eighth century before Christ in the following epilogue to the *Nirukta* (XIII.12.13):

Concerning the *mantras*, none can claim to have perceived their truths if one is not a seer... When seers passed beyond, men asked the gods, 'Who are going to be seers for us?' To them the gods gave reason [*tarka*] as the seer. And hence, whatever one speaks with reason, *following the track of the Word*, becomes as good as the utterance of a seer.[23]

The appeal to *tarka* is scintillating but its effulgence reflects the brilliance of the Vedas.

The view was also developed that if a smṛti practice was not found in the Vedas it was based on a Vedic text lost to us![24] In effect then smrti usage becomes supreme in such a case. In other texts the usages of the competent and virtuous people was given primacy. The *Āpastamba Dharma Sūtra* (I.7.20.6) declares:

> Righteousness and unrighteousness do not go about and say: 'This is righteousness, this is unrighteousness.' But what the *Ārya*-s praise when it is done, that is righteousness; what they blame, that is unrighteousness. One shall follow in one's conduct the conduct of well-behaved, aged, self-possessed, not greedy and not hypocritical *Ārya*-s which is unanimously approved in all countries.[25]

In this sense '*Dharma* is not established by deduction or revelation but is radically empirical',[26] but how radically empirical can one get? The conscience of even one ascetic is enough to pronounce on it, for according to Yājñavalkya (I.9) 'even one who is the best among knowers of spiritual matters (ascetics)... what he declares would be the right course of conduct'.[27] This accords rather well with Mahatma Gandhi finding himself on occasion in the minority of one!

V

There is another approach for determining dharma. And thereby hangs a tale. The tale is a famous one. The five Pāṇḍava brothers find themselves, in the course of their wanderings in the forest, desperately thirsty and by turns go out in search of water, each failing to return. Finally, Yudhiṣṭhira sets out himself and espies a lovely lake beside which he finds his brothers lying dead, as it were. At this sight Yudhiṣṭhira is overwhelmed with grief, and wonders what catastrophe could possibly have overtaken his brothers. Even though Yudhiṣṭhira is described in the text at this point as the 'mighty-armed and high-souled one, acquainted with the divisions of time and place' he could not solve the puzzle. As he saw no signs of any bodily injuries on his brothers he was inclined to attribute their death to Yama 'who in due time bringeth about the end of all things'. Having reached this despairing conclusion, Yudhiṣṭhira then proceeded to perform his ablutions in the lake. However, as he was about to do so, he was stopped by a voice which identified itself as a Yakṣa or semi-divine being, which claimed dominion over the body of water and which informed Yudhiṣṭhira that his brothers had been rendered unconscious by this celestial superintendent of the waters for trespassing on his domain. The Yakṣa declared:

> I am a crane, living on tiny fish. It is by me that thy younger brothers have been brought under the sway of the lord of departed spirits. If, thou, O prince, answer not the questions put by me, even thou shalt number the fifth corpse. Do not, O child, act rashly! This lake hath already been in my possession. Having answered my questions first, do thou, O Kunti's son, drink and carry away (as much as thou requirest)![28]

Yudhiṣṭhira took some time to identify the disembodied voice he heard as belonging to the Yakṣa and then 'approaching the Yakṣa who had spoken then, stood there. And that bull among the Bharatas [i.e. Yudhiṣṭhira], then beheld that Yakṣa of unusual eyes and huge body, tall like a palmyra-palm and looking like fire or the Sun, and irresistible and gigantic like a mountain, staying on a tree, and uttering a loud roar deep as that of the clouds. And the Yakṣa said, "These thy brothers, O king, repeatedly forbidden by me, would forcibly take away water. It is for this that they have been slain by me! He that wisheth to live, should not, O king, drink this water! O son of Pritha, act not rashly! This lake hath already been in my possession. Do thou, O son of Kunti, first answer my questions, and then take away as much as thou likest!" Yudhiṣṭhira said, "I do not, O Yakṣa, covet, what is already in thy possession! O bull among male beings, virtuous persons never approve that one should applaud his own self (without boasting, I shall, therefore, answer thy questions, according to my intelligence). Do thou ask me!"'[29]

The Yakṣa then asks Yudhiṣṭhira several questions whose number depends on the edition of the *Mahābhārata* we happen to be reading. But according to the text commented on by the medieval scholar Nīlakaṇṭha, Yudhiṣṭhira's oral exam ends on the following note: 'Who is truly happy? What is most wonderful? What is *the* path? What is *the* news? Answer these four questions of mine and let thy dead brothers revive.'

We are perhaps interested in knowing the answers to all the

four questions; and some of the readers may even know them already, but I would like to focus on only one of them, namely, what is *the* path? Yudhiṣṭhira's answer is contained in a famous verse which may be translated as follows:

(1) The Śrutis differ among themselves; (2) The Smṛtis differ among themselves; (3) The Sages differ among themselves; (4) The essence of Dharma is concealed in a cave; (5) Follow the path adopted by the *mahājana.*

We notice that with each line or segment of the verse each of the traditional sources of dharma has been progressively eliminated. The Śruti is self-discrepant—there go the Vedas; Smṛtis are contradictory—there go the Law books; the Sages differ regarding the norms of conduct among themselves and cancel each other out. But what of conscience? The essence of dharma is concealed deep in a cave, in an inaccessible region. I take this to imply that it may be too remote and subtle to be within the reach of even conscience. Now that all the traditional sources of dharma have been discarded, how do we identify it? The answer is provided in the last line: Follow the mahājana.

The current Hindi meaning of the term mahājana is money-lender but that leaves us short-changed. The simple direct Sanskrit meaning would seem to be 'a great person': 'Therefore that alone is the path which the great have trod.'[30] This makes sense and the matter can come to rest here. And who is better qualified to be called a mahājana in our times than Mahatma Gandhi—we can even say that we may not be Pāṇḍavas but he was the Yudhiṣṭhira of our times!

It seems then that we may have arrived at a proper resolution of the source of the dharma for us by filtering the sources of the dharma identified by Manu through the sieve of the answers provided by Yudhiṣṭhira to the Yakṣa's question—and in the end are left with the one holding the sieve, Yudhiṣṭhira himself. And why not? Is he not identified as the son of Dharma himself? And is not Mahatma Gandhi's arrival on the Indian scene something like the return of Yudhiṣṭhira, considering the moral quality and clarity he imparted to the movement for Independence. The stirring words of Pandit Nehru deserve to be quoted at length at this point:

Political freedom took new shape then and acquired a new content. Much that he said we only partially accepted or sometimes did not accept at all. But all this was secondary. The essence of his teaching was fearlessness and truth and action allied to these, always keeping the welfare of the masses in view. The greatest gift for an individual or a nation, so we have been told in our ancient books, was *abhaya*, fearlessness, not merely bodily courage but the absence of fear from the mind. Janaka and Yajnavalka had said, at the dawn of our history, that it was the function of the leaders of a people to make them fearless. But the dominant impulse in India under British rule was that of fear. Pervasive, oppressing, strangling fear; fear of the army, the police, the widespread secret service; fear of the official class; fear of laws meant to suppress, and of prison; fear of the landlord's agent, fear of the moneylender; fear of unemployment and starvation, which were always on the threshold. It was against this all-pervading fear that Gandhi's quiet and determined voice was raised: Be not afraid.

Was it so simple as all that? Not quite. And yet fear builds its phantoms which are more fearsome than reality itself and reality when calmly analyzed and its consequences willingly accepted loses much of its terror.

So, suddenly as it were, that black pall of fear was lifted from the people's shoulders, not wholly, of course, but to an amazing degree. As fear is close companion to falsehood, so truth follows fearlessness. The Indian people did not become much more truthful than they were, nor did they change their essential nature overnight; nevertheless a sea change was visible as the need for falsehood and furtive behavior lessened. It was a psychological change, almost as if some expert in psychoanalytical method had probed deep into the patient's past, found out the origins of his complexes, exposed them to his view, and thus rid him of that burden.[31]

And is not that light still capable of guiding us? To quote Nehru again, this time on Mahatma Gandhi's exit rather than entrance:

The light has gone out of our lives... Yet I am wrong, for the light that shone in this country was no ordinary light ... and a thousand years later that light will still be seen in this country and the world will see it. For that light represented the living truth.[32]

I would like to build the case for Mahatma Gandhi as the mahājana for our times further. But you might wonder, as I do, what role do reason and conscience play in the foregoing discussion? What source of law did Ekanātha utilize when 'on one occasion he gave to the pariahs the food, the food he had specially prepared as an offering to his forefathers' and on another 'poured holy water that he had brought from Godāvarī a great distance away, down the throat of a dying ass'?[33] Here we have the conscience of the reformer turning the tables, in fact, like the overturning of the tables of the moneylenders by Jesus within the precincts of the temple. I think the authors of Hindu law often overlook the person who stands outside it sometimes as an ultimate point of reference. He can be either the saint-scholar, the swāmī or the guru. Thus the means of valid knowledge, the *pramāṇas*, play their own role in the context,[34] but as the swāmī has renounced the world, he thereby stands on the Archimedean ground from where he can move it. How else can we explain the social impact of the swamis, especially in modern Hinduism. The guru is even more influential in this way. Though his disciple may belong to the social order, the guru in some sense stands above it and the disciple is supposed to follow his behest howsoever inscrutable it might appear. Nisargadatta Maharaj, the so-called Bidi-Swami of Bombay insisted that 'no one ... could know the motives behind the actions of a truly realized *guru*'. To illustrate his point he told 'the story of a *saṁyāsin* (world-renouncing ascetic) who was told by his *guru* to marry. He obeyed and suffered bitterly. But all four of his children became the greatest saints and *ṛṣis* of Maharashtra',[35] namely, Nivṛttinātha, Jñānadeva, Sopānadeva and Muktābai.[36]

There is the guru as the conscience and then there is also the conscience as the guru, overriding all other constraints as when Rāmānuja chose to share the salvific eight-syllabled Vaiṣṇava mantra, esoterically received by him, with a larger audience than was ever intended by his guru.[37] To talk about Hindu law without reason and conscience, is like talking of the American Civil War without mentioning slavery or of the Second World War without mentioning the Holocaust. It can be done, but can it, really?

B. K. Matilal poses the issue of the exceptional individual in an interesting way. He asks: Why are we shocked by moral misdeeds when they are associated with Kṛṣṇa and not shocked when they are committed by the Kauravas? After suggesting that this may be because we had higher expectations of Kṛṣṇa, he goes on to say: 'There may be another way of looking at this issue. Let us regard Kṛṣṇa as a moral agent here. It was his duty to uphold *dharma* which also included justice, at any cost. The exact nature of *dharma* has remained ever elusive, for it was never spelled out fully.' On the one hand it is the elusive nature of dharma which is often emphasized while on the other it is sometimes identified with the 'rigid moral code of a given society'. This sets up a creative tension between its divergent understandings but these understandings, though divergent are not incoherent, though contrary are not contradictory. The elusive subtlety of dharma ensures that its 'rigidity can sometimes be challenged by a proper agent who has proven to be superior to others in the community both in talents and intelligence as well as in leadership qualities. This only acknowledges the possibility of what is today called "a paradigm shift". Sometimes it is possible for a leader to transcend or breach the rigid code of conduct valued in the society, with the sole idea of creating a new paradigm that will also be acknowledged and esteemed within that order. Our Kṛṣṇa might be looked upon as a leader of that sort.'[38]

So also Mahatma Gandhi. He not only shifted the paradigm. He did much more. He lifted it.

VI

I tried to argue above that, utilizing the Hindu sources of dharma as resources for our thinking about Hinduism for our age, it could be plausibly argued that Gandhian Hinduism is paradigmatic for our times; and that in the Gandhian paradigm of Hinduism the concepts of varṇa and religious tolerance as understood by Gandhi were key elements—key in the sense not only of unlocking the secrets of Hinduism as it were but also constituting the key which Hinduism was to provide to the world, to open the door into the future. Before I proceed any further I think one needs to extend the discussion of these two aspects of Gandhian thought a little further. Of the two, it is the Gandhian understanding of the Hindu concept of varṇa which seems to particularly require elaboration and even clarification, as it can be easily misunderstood.

Gandhi's view of varṇa is best illustrated by contrasting it with the 'caste system' as such, as he saw prevailing around him, which consisted of the following four features: (1) occupation based on birth; (2) the world of social interaction with the marriage pool and the breaking of bread also based on birth; (3) a hierarchical arrangement of the units defining (1) and (2); (4) untouchability.

Mahatma Gandhi rejected untouchability outright as also any sense of inferiority or superiority based on caste-affiliation. About untouchability he declared, 'True, Hinduism does not regard untouchability as a sin' but 'Hinduism has sinned in giving sanction to untouchability'.[39] On the question of caste hierarchy he declared, invoking the metaphor of the *puruṣa-sūkta*: 'If they are members of one body, how can they be superior or inferior to another.'[40] If there was any superiority it was in the matter of 'capacity for superior service, but not superior status'.[41] Though he initially remained essentially conservative in matters of intermarriage and interdining, he gradually broadened his horizons in these respects.

The one point on which Gandhi refused to yield was that of occupation based on birth. He states unequivocally: 'It does attach to birth. A man cannot change his varna by choice.'[42] His conversation with an American clergyman is worth citing in this respect.

Q. In your Hinduism do you basically include the caste system?

A. I do not. Hinduism does not believe in caste. I would obliterate it at once. But I believe in *Varna Dharma* which is the law of life. I believe that some people are born to teach and some to defend and some to engage in trade and agriculture and some to do manual labour, so much so that these occupations become hereditary. The law of *varna* is nothing but the law of conservation of energy. Why should my son not be a scavenger if I am one?

Indeed? Do you go so far?

I do, because I hold the scavenger's profession in no way inferior to a clergyman's.

I grant that, but should Lincoln have been a wood-chopper rather than President of the U.S.A.?

> But why should not a wood-chopper be a President of the United States? Gladstone used to chop wood.
>
> But he did not accept it as his calling.
>
> He would not have been worse off if he had done so. What I mean is, one born a scavenger must earn his livelihood by being a scavenger, and then do whatever else he likes. For a scavenger is as worthy of his hire as a lawyer or your President. That, according to me, is Hinduism. There is no better communism on earth, and I have illustrated it with one verse from the *Upanishads* which means: 'God pervades all—animate and inanimate. Therefore, renounce all and dedicate it to God and then live.' The right of living is thus derived from renunciation. It does not say, 'When all do their part of the work I too will do it.' It says, 'Don't bother about others, do your job first and leave the rest to HIM.' *Varna Dharma* acts even as the law of gravitation. I cannot cancel it or its working by trying to jump higher and higher day by day till gravitation ceases to work. That effort will be vain. So is the effort to jump over one another. The law of *varna* is the antithesis of competition which kills.[43]

As to the inevitable question: What if a person's natural abilities were inconsistent with the birth-ascribed varṇa, Gandhi's answer was as striking as it was simple. A person was only entitled to earn his livelihood through his varṇa duties; if he possessed other gifts it was equally his duty to offer them to society free of charge. He must never earn his livelihood through them, only through his varṇa vocation.

Mahatma Gandhi's views on religious tolerance, as implied in his opposition to religious conversion, are too well known and need not be explained, but they can be embellished in the light of the story of Yudhiṣṭhira's encounter with the Yakṣa. We concluded our earlier narration of the encounter between the Yakṣa and Yudhiṣṭhira with the Yakṣa's promise that if Yudhiṣṭhira answered the last four questions satisfactorily all his brothers would be revived. It does happen, but not before another twist in the narrative. It will be helpful to recall here that of his four brothers Bhīma and Arjuna, like him, were the sons of Kuntī while Nakula and Sahadeva were really step-brothers being the sons of Mādrī, the other wife of his father Pāṇḍu.

After the questions had been asked by the Yakṣa and answered by Yudhiṣṭhira, the Yakṣa initially promised to revive only one of his brothers and asked him to specify the one he wished to see revived. This reminds one of the choice faced by some of the victims of the Jewish Holocaust but the situation here, though equally serious, was fortunately not that grim. To the surprise of the Yakṣa, Yudhiṣṭhira passed over Bhīma and Arjuna—who were not only strong and brave respectively but also his blood brothers—and asked that Nakula be revived. This led the puzzled Yakṣa to ask another question, though more out of curiosity rather than to test Yudhiṣṭhira's virtuous knowledge: '...why dost thou wish Nakula to revive?'[44] Yudhiṣṭhira answered: 'My father had two wives, Kunti and Madri. Let them both have children. This is what I wish. As Kunti is to me, so also is Madri. There is no difference in my eye. I desire to act equally towards my mothers. [If I live then Kunti's line will survive]. Therefore, let Nakula live [so that Madri's line may also survive]'. At this the Yakṣa was so pleased, or shall we say moved, by Yudhiṣṭhira's compassion that he revived all the brothers. And so our narrative does have a story-book ending.

Earlier on the relationship of a follower to his religion had been compared to that of a child to his or her mother, in terms of the Gandhian view of this relationship. If that metaphor is transferred to the present narrative, it produces an astounding and wholesome result: that the follower of one religion may choose to save another religion from extinction, over the lives of the followers of his own! Needless to say, the allusion is fraught with an unexpectedly edifying relevance for the current situation in our country.

It is my painful duty, however, to descend from the lofty moral heights to which the juxtaposition of a Yudhiṣṭhira with a Mahatma Gandhi had exalted us, and to remind ourselves that forty-six years have passed since Mahatma Gandhi laid down his life, in a manner gloriously reminiscent of another nailed down almost two thousand years ago. Given this passage of time one is compelled to ask: Does the Gandhian paradigm still hold for Hinduism or is it now generating such cognitive dissonance as calls for the first gropings towards another?

The 'colossal caprice' of history produced a Gandhi; there is no one around in the contemporary Hindu world of comparable stature, or even one possessing a significantly diminished stature. But could we then not follow him? Non-Gandhians will, of course, not follow him but even as Gandhians we may not, for Gandhi repudiated Gandhism in no uncertain terms:

> There is no such thing as 'Gandhism', and I do not want to leave any sect after me. I do not claim to have originated any new principle or doctrine. I have simply tried in my own way to apply the eternal truths to our daily life and problems. There is, therefore, no question of my leaving any code like the *Code of Manu.* There can be no comparison between that great lawgiver and me. The opinions I have formed and the conclusions I have arrived at are not final. I may change them tomorrow. I have nothing new to teach the world. Truth and non-violence are as old as the hills. All I have done is to try experiments in both on as vast a scale as I could do.[45]

We had begun to talk in terms of paradigm shifts but what is the point in talking of them if there is no one who can shift it? Perhaps the way the paradigm is to be shifted in Hinduism now itself requires a paradigm shift! I have to begin groping sooner than I had bargained for but perhaps it is better to grope than to merely hope.

VII

A reconsideration of Yudhiṣṭhira's reply to the Yakṣa's question—namely that the Śrutis differ; the Smṛtis differ; there is no uniquely authoritative single sage; the essence of dharma is inaccessible: and therefore the path to take is the one taken by the mahājana—requires us to revert to a consideration of the term mahājana at this point. The word mahājana can mean either (1) a great person or (2) a great number of persons. Although the first sense is the obvious one, tradition, in this context, favours the second sense, an understanding which is surprisingly logical. If it has already been asserted that the sages, who were great persons, differ among themselves, then how does the great man, the *mahānjana*, help us overcome the dilemma? The point then is that if contradiction is to be avoided, as in a previous line the sages, who are or were presumably great persons, are declared to be at odds regarding dharma, the sense of a 'great number of persons' must be favoured. To put the matter succinctly: consensus is the arbiter of dharma.[46]

The second sense, though *less* obvious is therefore the *more* plausible one, and this point is important for the argument. Lest this preference be considered idiosyncratic it is worth bearing in mind that this is how P.V. Kane translates the term. He renders the entire verse as follows (from a text in which the first line reads *tarko 'pratiṣṭaḥ*):

> rationalisation is unstable, Vedas are in conflict with each other, there is no single sage whose opinion is held to be authoritative (by all), the truth about Dharma is enveloped in a cave (i.e. it cannot be clearly discerned) and that therefore the path (to be followed) is the one followed by the great mass of people.[47]

He also points out that Śaṅkara has employed the word in this sense in his gloss on *Brahmasūtra* IV.2.7. In fact Nīlakaṇṭha, in the sixteenth century, in his commentary on this verse takes it clearly in this sense; for he glosses it as *bahujanasammatamityarthah.* The late Professor B.K. Matilal tentatively offered the sense as an open possibility, which is *my* unhesitating choice also.

It is a point of some if not great interest here that, if the rendering of mahājana as the masses is correct, Yudhiṣṭhira's position accords primacy to a point of view which has prevailed for quite some time, in one form or another, in Hindu legal circles. For instance, even Manu says explicitly (IV.176) that one should avoid that dharma which will end in unhappiness or is considered offensive by the people (*lokavikruṣṭa*). Manu is not alone in this and is supported by Yājñavalkya and others.[48] P.V. Kane pertinently points out that the word used is 'lokavikruṣṭa (hated or reviled by the people) and not "siṣṭavikruṣṭa", the idea being that even if orthodox learned *pundits* insist that people must follow what the Vedas and smṛtis declare to be dharma, common people may give up practices condemned by them or hateful to them'.[49]

This distinction between *siṣṭa* and *loka* seems to go beyond, the one posited by P.V. Kane between what the 'orthodox learned pundits' insist on and what the people in general approve or disapprove. According to the *Taittrīya Upaniṣad*, for instance, being even an orthodox Brahmin is not enough, for it is the conduct not of Brahmins but of *virtuous* Brahmins which is supposed to dispel doubts about dharma. The text says (I.11.4):

4. Then, if there is in you any doubt regarding any deeds, any doubt regarding conduct, you should behave yourself in such matters, as the Brāhmanas there (who are) competent to judge, devoted (to good deeds), not led by others, not harsh, lovers of virtue would behave in such cases.[50]

If one bears in mind the fact that the *Mahābhārata* in which this statement regarding mahājana occurs, is said to have been *specially* composed with the Śūdras and women in mind, who are denied accessibility to the Vedas in classical Hinduism, the point gains in potency.[51] It reinforces the broader understanding of mahājana, as it further tilts the scale in favour of loka over siṣṭa. This ties into the sacred history of Hinduism, as the events of the *Mahābhārata* constitute the cusp between the Dvāpara and Kali, our own *yuga*, which could be interpreted as belonging to the śūdras.[52] Mahatma Gandhi's plea that all Hindus should consider and declare themselves to be śūdras was not based on an egalitarian whim;[53] it is firmly founded on our common political subjugation in secular history. Those, for whom the mythical nature of the yuga argument does not diminish its cultural force in terms of Hindu sacred history, the point holds good with even greater force. It may be added that the usages described as not permitted in Kali Yuga[54] include those which came to be disapproved by the masses on moral, compassionate and egalitarian grounds.[55]

From this point onwards the argument can be developed in two directions: backward and forward; backward towards the Upaniṣads and forward towards the sociology of religion.

First a backward glance. The story is told in the *Kena Upaniṣad* of how, when the gods once defeated the non-gods, they began to harbour the conceit that they had done so on their own. Then too a Yakṣa appeared at whose bidding Agni and Vāyu were unable to burn or blow a blade of grass respectively.

Umā identified that Yakṣa, for the discombobulated gods, as Brahman—the ultimate reality. Is it a mere coincidence that just as the Yakṣa was the catalyst for the realization by the gods of the basis of reality, the ultimate *truth*, in the episode discussed from the *Mahābhārata* he was the catalyst for the affirmation by Yudhiṣṭhira of ultimate *virtue*—or rather its source, which consists of the verdict of the masses as opposed to the classes, not to say elites?

I would now like to move forward with the extension of a Weberian insight that 'religions are not shaped by *all* the followers of a particular faith (each adherent, carrying as it were equal weight), but that certain groups are particularly strategic at certain times and under certain circumstances'.[56] Weber himself identified the 'primary carriers' of the world religions as follows:

> In Confucianism, the world-organizing bureaucrat; in Hinduism, the world-ordering magician; in Buddhism, the mendicant monk wandering through the world; in Islam, the warrior seeking to conquer the world; in Judaism, the wandering trader; and in Christianity, the itinerant journeyman.[57]

In keeping with Yudhiṣṭhira's insight I would plead that all followers should have an equal hand in the shaping of their faith—or at least have an equal opportunity to do so—that there may be principally (if there must be functionally) no distinction between primary and secondary carriers of a tradition, so far as Hinduism is concerned. *The great challenge Hinduism faces in our times is to ensure for all Hindus an equal opportunity in determining what Hinduism should be for our times.* How this might be accomplished, is for the reader to decide.

Chapter 2

Karma and Rebirth Today

I

I shall begin with a story. If you have already heard it, just pretend you haven't. It is said that when wives laugh at the worn-out wisecracks of their husbands, they do so not because the jokes are smart but because they are.

When he went off to battle, a certain army officer kept his money—two thousand rupees—in trust with a Rawalpindi merchant who was under contract to supply rations to the troops. One day during the Kabul uprising, the officer was killed under bizarre circumstances: he was unable to stop the mare he was riding from heading directly into the enemy lines. No matter how hard he reined in the usually trustworthy animal, she would not alter her deadly course, and a hail of fire killed both horse and rider.

The government sent the officer's belongings to his relatives, who knew nothing about the sum of money he had left with the merchant. The merchant, for his part, mentioned the money to no one, and kept it as if it were his own.

Twenty years later he was living in Saharanpur, running a small shop. One night, as he was entertaining some old friends, his guests heard sobs and piteous cries coming from the next room. The merchant explained that this was his daughter-in-law, mourning her husband who had died only a few days before. The guests offered their condolences, but expressed surprise that the merchant was entertaining them when he, too, should be mourning his son's death. In reply, the merchant told them the following story:

'Twenty years ago, after my return from Rawalpindi, I married, and my wife gave birth to a son. When he had grown up, we arranged a marriage for him, but immediately after the wedding he became gravely ill, and nothing we did would cure him. Finally, I brought in a Muslim clergyman to try to heal him. The clergyman recited some words and I immediately gave him two and one half rupees, which was all I had in my pocket at that moment. I then asked my son how he felt. He said that he was about to die and he explained.

"Twenty years ago," he told me, "I left two thousand rupees in your safekeeping just before I was killed in the Kabul uprising. You kept the money, and so I was reborn as your son to recover it. The two and one half rupees you had in your pocket were all that was left of that money, and when you passed them on to the priest in payment for the services he had rendered to me, our account was squared.

"The mare that rode so wilfully directly into enemy lines was reborn as my wife, and because of the way in which she made me die, she will have to grieve at my passing. That will square my account with her."

'So,' the merchant said, 'the officer is dead and the mare is crying. For whom should I mourn, the mare or the officer? Therefore, gentlemen, be good enough to enjoy your meal.'[1]

II

As might have been surmised by now, I now intend to speak about karma and rebirth in Hinduism. To an Australian aborigine, the operation of the boomerang could well symbolize the operation of karma. In other words, what you give is what you get; what you send out is what you receive back; the way you treat others is the way you get treated. One might protest that this is not the way the world is, where the virtuous suffer and the wicked prosper. In the face of this *immediate* fact the doctrine of karma asserts the *ultimately* just nature of the universe. The expression 'ultimate' is important. We say, for instance, that justice prevails in the state of Quebec. Does it mean that no theft or robbery, no crime is committed in Quebec. Quite obviously crime is committed in Quebec. What it really means is that when crime is committed the criminals are apprehended and brought to book. The principle of justice implies not the absence of the violation of law but the principle of its ultimate assertion after a phase of its apparent lapse. So is it with karma. Karma is payback. This basic concept of karma can be enunciated in many ways: that just as causes have effects, actions have consequences; that life goes on so long as there is 'unfinished business'; that what goes around comes around; things take time; God's mills grind slowly but they grind exceedingly fine.

The doctrine seems to have been designed to answer three

major questions: Why am I who I am and not somebody else? Why does what happens to me happen to me and not something else? And why does what happens to me happens to me and not to somebody else ('why me'?). In this chapter I would like to focus only on these three aspects. I shall first present the traditional views on these points and towards the end I would like to present an interpretation suitable for our own times.

The first aspect of karma relates to the time-honoured controversy between free will and fate. On this issue at least three different positions are found within the tradition, all associated with the doctrine of karma. At one end of the spectrum one encounters the view that everything is predetermined, is fated; at the other end of the spectrum one encounters the view that as all karma is originally voluntary; all that really exists is only free will, a will we can continuously exercise as we wish. Then there is the middle position that both fate and free will operate in life and what actually happens is the product of past karma interacting with present karma.

An example from daily life will help illustrate this point of view. I do not smoke—but I can, of my free will, commence smoking whenever I wish. In this sense I possess free will. If, however, I have been smoking heavily for fifteen years and have developed symptoms of lung cancer, then I must undergo the effects of my persistent smoking. It is fate. I still have free will—I can give up smoking—but it will no longer check my cancer which has become a force in itself. But let us suppose I have been smoking for five years and the surgeon-general's warning has its due effect on me and I decide to give up smoking. Now whether I will be able to abide by my decision depends on the operation of two forces, the force of habit which is the outcome of my past karma and the force of the resolve to quit smoking, the force of my present karma. Whether I will pick up a cigarette or not depends on the balance of these forces. It seems to me that this middle position is the one which accords better with our experience of life. There is a certain givenness in life, one may be tall or short, fair or dark; but there is also an openness, one may start on a new course of action if one chooses to do so, acquire a new skill or read a new book, or learn a new language, and so on. This third view emphasizes the role of effort in life and is therefore wholesome. It also indicates that *past* karma is best used as a residual rather than an initial explanation. When all efforts have been exhausted and a situation cannot be changed, only then may it be attributed to past karma. If a person falls ill, then only if after every possible treatment the illness turns out to be incurable may it be attributed to past karma. This seems to be the basis of the classification of certain diseases in Hindu texts as curable (*sādhya*), curable with difficulty (*kaṣṭasādhya*) and incurable (*asādhya*).

Not only does karma allow for three possible views of fate and free will, it is also seen as operating in multiple dimensions and I shall use Sanskrit words to represent some of these dimensions. These words are *phala*, *saṁskāra* and *jāti*. Let me use the example of smoking once again to illustrate these dimensions.

First phala. When I smoke the inhalation produces certain predictable and, in its own way, inevitable consequences in the form of the effect of nicotine on lungs, etc. These are the natural or mechanical consequences of our acts which must follow as night follows day. This is the natural dimension of karma. In its moral version it means that good deeds must inevitably produce favourable results and evil deeds likewise must generate adverse results.

Next saṁskāra. The word refers to mental impressions, specially ingrained mental impressions. Every time I smoke the act of smoking produces natural biological effects. But that is not all—something also happens to my psyche. Every time I smoke I strengthen my proclivity to smoke. An act repeatedly carried out becomes a habit, and a constellation of habits constitutes character. This is the psychological or mental dimension of karma.

But this is not all. When I smoke I turn those sitting around me into passive smokers. Thus my karma of smoking has a communal aspect to it also. And if my nicotine addiction is passed on to my children, the consequences of my actions no longer remain confined to me, but become generational. I have used the word jāti, taking the cue from Manu, to refer to this communal and generational, or should we say extra-personal, dimension of karma. This dimension of karma has been relatively neglected in traditional discussions of karma. The emphasis on individual rights in modern law, according to some, has led to the neglect of communal rights. It seems that in ancient India, liberation from karma was viewed in the main as getting personally liberated from karma; such a soteriological approach may account for the relative neglect of the communal dimension of karma. However, the Hinduism of our times will have to remedy this neglect, specially as the modern world has become increasingly interdependent. In an ancient world in which villages functioned as self-contained units, such a unitary understanding of karma may have sufficed but considering the nexus societies and nations form today, it is hard even for those seeking liberation perhaps to be 'islands unto themselves' for even more so now than earlier 'no man is an island'. Even medieval Hinduism recognized this dimension in the spiritual sphere in the concept of *satsaṅga* and ancient Hinduism through the formation of *maṭhas* for communal living. The development of jātis as social categories also testifies to an awareness of the communal dimension. But in our times the fact gains a significance all its own.

Normally one is supposed to be born in a particular jāti on account of one's karma—that is to say, individual action determines one's communal destiny. I think this principle could be extended in two directions: (1) an individual action also affects the community's destiny, community being redefined as the social unit of which one is an integral part, as when living in a student residence or hostel, a matter which *used* to be decided by one's birth. However, if this etymological anachronism trailing behind it is overlooked, the point becomes clear. After all, the individual's behaviour always had consequences for the social unit or jāti, otherwise what need was there to excommunicate anyone, including Gandhi! The principle of karma at the level of jāti enables us to realize that the consequences of our actions affect not just us but others as well; that when we actively smoke we turn others into passive smokers. (2) The other direction in which the interpretation of karma along the lines of jāti can be extended is not only pragmatic but also moral—the two strands braided by us in explicating the doctrine. The *Mahābhārata* mentions an ascetic, Kauśika by name, who was known for his veracity, but finally had to go to hell under the following circumstances. While he was engaged in penance in the forest, some robbers came upon him in hot pursuit of their would-be victims. Kauśika, when asked, truthfully pointed out the direction in which they had gone. The robbers caught up with their intended victims and killed them and the bad karma of the killing fell to Kauśika's share.[2] So in the end Kauśika was thrown into hell. This story was narrated to Arjuna by Kṛṣṇa as a warning against a purely formal approach to ethics. I would like to use it here to illustrate the point how general good (*lokasaṅgraha*) may require the sacrifice of personal morality, narrowly conceived.

When we extend our horizon from jāti or 'our people' to loka or 'our world' in general, it becomes possible to integrate a psychological insight into our conceptual revisioning of karma. Psychologists, and many of us who are observers of the human psyche, have noticed that we tend to treat others the way we are treated. Child-abuse, for instance, runs in families. We might extend the doctrine of karma to embrace the idea that not only do we get treated the way we treat others retributively, but that we also treat *others* the way we are treated—only that the *other* in this case is not always the perpetrator of that action upon us but somebody other than him or her who may have had little to do with it. Call it transference of sorts. In fact, it is a form of karmic transference—but distributive rather than retributive. We begin to treat others *generally* in accordance with how we may have been treated *personally*, which takes us beyond the one-to-one equation commonly advanced in such cases in standard presentations of karma. In my view this enlarges rather than supplants our traditional understanding of karma: that the agent of an act ultimately becomes its patient or that the subject becomes the object. Who, after all, are *we*? What are the sources of our self? Is not the world around us implicated in our self-identity? Just as the principle of karma constitutes the principle of unity in the multiplicity of our actions, it may also constitute the principle of unity in the psychological complexity of our existence. The traditional formulation of the karmic question is: What is the consequence of my action for me? The reformulation I suggest asks two further questions: What is the consequence of my actions for others as well as for me, and further: Why do I act the way I do? Thus, a more comprehensive calculus as a whole for karma is being advocated; a more communal eschatology and a more broad-based etiology of karma is being sought.

In the course of our discussion of the traditional material on karma I suggested that the Hinduism for our times may favour that view which sees life as involving an interaction of both fate and free will and the view which incorporates the communal dimension of karma. Let me offer the rationale for suggesting why this is appropriate for *our times.* We are now a politically independent people. We have been so for over forty years now. In earlier times we were a subject people, when our lives were affected by decisions taken not by us but by others who ruled over us. It is obvious that such a state of affairs would affect the thinking of the Hindus on karma. The absence of the power of decision-making would lead them towards a fatalistic interpretation of karma and the social disruption caused by foreign invasions would lead people to an individualistic interpretation of karma in an atmosphere in which 'each is for himself and devil take the hindmost'.

Thus, the doctrine of karma in the context of our own times should be interpreted with a greater emphasis on the principle of effort it implies. Political independence translates into personal independence. A wag remarked on seeing the Leaning Tower of Pisa: What avails it if you have the inclination but not the time? Hinduism says in effect: If you have the inclination, you have the time. The universe is a cosmic Santa Claus, but its gifts are not gratis, they are obtained through the coupons of effort. Karma represents the search for perfection through effort and it is in this context alone that astrology makes any sense to me. The urge to achieve must have been so strong that when faced with failure the ancient Hindus, I speculate, may have asked themselves: How did things go wrong when we did everything right? Are there some occult forces at work we did not take into account? The problem with many of us is that we make astrology the first rather than the last resort.

In interpreting the doctrine of karma for our times the need for a fuller recognition of its social dimension must also be emphasized. The rigidification of the caste system seems to have represented cellular defence on the part of the Hindu body politic against invasive presences—but the cells then became calcified: karma becomes dharma in its narrowest individualistic sense. Now once again karma should be linked with dharma, and dharma must be reinterpreted beyond the upholding of individual roles or roles of smaller units within society such as castes as that of upholding *society itself as a whole.* In addition to these, there are three other directions in which it might be appropriate to move the contemporary Hindu understanding of karma.

(1) Once it is realized that one is the master of one's karma—through effort—and not vice versa, it becomes possible to view karma in a broader perspective. The doctrine of karma no more prevents us from acting freely than the law of gravitation prevents us from moving around freely. But just as one can break through the field of gravity, one can rise above past karma through accelerated present karma. This point has already been made, as also the point that karma is cumulative—that the effect of virtuous or diligent behaviour may only become visible over a period of time rather than being immediately apparent. What needs to be recognized is that compassion overrides karma both on an egoistic as well as altruistic view of things. If we see someone suffering and do nothing to help the person by adopting the view that 'that is his karma', expressing in Hindu jargon the Western attitude that 'that is his problem', then one has to remember that when it is our turn to suffer, we

too will receive no succour on the same argument that it is our karma. But if we help others when they suffer we too will be helped when we suffer. There is a tendency to reconcile ourselves to the suffering of others by blaming it on their karma and to forget our dharma to help others. It is said that when Mahatma Gandhi told his mentor Raychandbhai 'people suffer because of their bad karma', the compassion of his mentor forced him to ask Gandhi: 'But why do people perform bad karma?' According to the altruistic view, even the entire calculus of karma can at times be dispensed with. It is said that when Rāmānuja was told by his guru that Rāmānuja might have to go to hell for revealing the salvific mantra, meant for esoteric transmission, to all and sundry, Ramanuja replied: 'It is true that I will go to hell but just think of all those who have been saved!'

(2) The doctrine of karma implies the view that we are responsible for what happens to us to a greater extent than may be immediately obvious to us. Socrates is believed to have said that the unexamined life is not worth living. A karmic interpretation of this statement could be that we should examine our own actions, our motives. The road not merely to virtue but to psychological health lies that way.

(3) But the aspect of karma on which I would like to place the maximum emphasis for our times is the principle of justice involved in it. The doctrine of karma suggests that the striving for justice is not merely a personal, a political or a socio-economic endeavour—it is a cosmic endeavour and we can be partners in it. After all, why do we have courts at all if we believe in karma. Why don't we let karma take care of things, and wait for the bad karma of the thieves to catch up with them. Instead, we try to institute justice and let karma take care of what falls through the cracks. It is in this interpretation of karma as justice—specially as social justice—that its understanding as effort, the recognition of its social dimension and its employment as a residual explanation, all coalesce.

III

In order to facilitate the transition to the next point I would like to restate the doctrine of karma minimally. 'As a Sanskrit proverb puts it: It may be a day, or a week, or a month, or a year, or another life, but the effect of one's actions must at some time be experienced.'[3]

Typically, the unit of time taken into consideration in the working out of karma has been 'another life'. However, when Philip H. Ashby interviewed students at the University of Andhra near Waltair in the 1970s, he found that the students wanted to make a clear distinction between 'karma that is passed from one existence over to a later existence and karma that is passed from one moment of life to another, later time in this same life'.[4] He also discovered that fifty-six per cent believed in both kinds of karma, 'while a large number who did not believe in karma as something carrying over from one life to another did hold that it is an active force in the successive stages of this present life'.[5]

This view may not be as novel as it appears at first sight. There is a story in the *Mahābhārata* in which an ascetic casts an angry look at a bird whose dropping fell on him and the bird was reduced to ashes by his irate glance. Thus, filled with conceit at his paranormal powers he went out to collect alms and when he cast an unpleasant glance at the tarrying housewife who had taken longer than he had expected to respond, she said coolly: 'I'm not a bird!' The story continues as to how, on being shocked that an ordinary housewife could excel an ascetic at his own game, he seeks out her teacher, only to be further shocked that this teacher earned his living by selling meat. But the ascetic, appearances to the contrary notwithstanding, engages in a dialogue on dharma with this *vyādha* or butcher and is so impressed by his virtues that when the discussion begins to extend to the other births this vyādha can recall, as the ascetic says (II.206. 10–12:[critical edition]):

[Why talk of being a Brahmin in other lives]. In my opinion you are a Brāhmana right now. No doubt need be entertained in this respect. A

Brahmin who born as one, pursues a vicious course of conduct, is a hypocrite and prone to evil is like a *śūdra* and that *sūdra* who is actively engaged in pursuing restraint, truth and virtue, him I consider a Brahmin. He becomes so by his conduct.

Manu also attests to how, in the course of the *same* life (II.172), 'a twice-born man, who, not having studied the Veda, applies himself to other (and worldly study) soon falls, even while living, to the condition of a *śūdra* and his descendants (after him)'.[6]

We know that a Hindu is not born; a Hindu is reborn; and we know that belief in rebirth and karma are closely associated in Hinduism as logical corollaries.[7] I would, therefore, like to offer an illustration which, while retaining the plausibility of karmic connection spread over several lives, yet shifts its focus to the karmic continuities within a life.

It is best to grasp the idea of several lives on the analogy of daily living. One day of our lives is connected with another. We start off in the morning where we left off at night—despite the interregnum of sleep. Similarly, we start off in one life where we leave off in another—despite the interval of death. Just as one day is linked to another so is one life to another. What we can or may do today cannot be dissociated from yesterday; but it may not be its mere replication either. There is a continuity which is dynamic and which allows for change. This gives to the everyday expression: live life from day to day, an unsuspected semantic potency!

With this in mind allow me to make two statements. The first is that whether we believe in an afterlife or not, the practical consequence of belief or disbelief in rebirth is the same. If this is the only life we have it must be lived to the hilt and we must try to achieve whatever we can. But if there is rebirth and the results of our actions carry over to the next then, again, we must do the same—for it is by making the most of this life that we best improve our prospects in the next. In both cases one must make the most of this life. Thus the practical implication of whichever meaning of karma one takes or whatever view of life or death one takes, it could be argued, is the same.

The second statement I would like to make is that in modern times what took several lives in the past can be achieved in one life. Let us suppose that the average life expectancy in ancient times was twenty-five years. In India, for instance, life-expectancy has risen from around 27 in 1948 to 60 or above in 1993. In other words *two lives are now contained in one!* Let us next consider the quality of life rather than its quantity. In the ancient world literacy was barely 2 per cent. Even in India it is now close to 50 per cent and many Western countries are close to achieving universal literacy. Next consider geographical mobility. People in the ancient world, when the doctrine of rebirth was formulated (was it formulated to compensate for a declining life span?), mostly lived and died in their own locality. But now when one goes to the West does one not hear oneself say—I am starting a *new life* in Canada. The ancient vision of someone dying in India and being reborn in Canada has its modern analogue in someone migrating from India to Canada. Thus the collective consequence of the characteristic features of modern life—longevity, literacy, mobility; and to which we may add technology and so on—is to compress several lives into one life. One should therefore promote the *idea of restructuring of our one life in the modern world in accordance with our aspirations as the modern counterpart to the seeking of favourable changes in fate and fortune over several lives in ancient India.*

IV

The doctrines of karma and of successive births or *saṁsāra* are regarded as characteristic of Hinduism though not specific to Hinduism, shared as they are, as a sort of common doctrinal property in one way or another, by the three other religions of India, Buddhism, Jainism and Sikhism. The concept of *mokṣa* or *mukti* or liberation falls in the same category. However, although the constellation of ideas represented by karma, saṁsāra and mukti are Indic rather than Hindu, there is a doctrine connecting the three which has come to be very strongly, if not exclusively, associated with Hinduism—and that is the doctrine of *karma yoga*, or to spell it out more fully, *niṣkāma karma yoga*. It is perhaps idle, if not captious, to say that the word niṣkāma does not occur in the *Bhagavadgītā*, for the concept certainly does. And it can hardly be gainsaid that the *Bhagavadgītā* has been the main vehicle for the propagation of this doctrine—and certainly in modern times, at the hands of Tilak and Gandhi.

I would like to elaborate on this movement in thought represented by the transformation of karma into karma yoga, on the transformation of karma as something which binds one to saṁsāra into a means out of it, when performed in the spirit of yoga, thereby confirming the optimistic Hindu aphorism that 'saṁsāra contains within it the seeds of its own destruction'.

The essence of karma yoga is said to lie in the performance of action without regard for its fruits, or duty for duty's sake, as it were. It is a doctrine closely bound with the idea of *sva-dharma* or one's duty. As M. Hiriyanna explains:

> If the idea of duty is thus separated from that of its consequences, it may appear that there will be no means of determining its content in any particular context in life, and that therefore the Gītā teaching, while it may tell us *how* to act, fails altogether to guide us as to *what* deeds we should do. But really there is no such lack of guidance in the teaching for according to it, the duties which a person has to undertake are determined by the place he occupies in society. This is another important principle enunciated in the Gītā, viz. that one's own duty (*sva-dharma*), be it ever so low, is superior to another's—a principle whose knowledge has filtered down even to the lowest ranks of our society as indicated, for instance, but the words which Kālidāsa puts into the mouth of the fisherman in the Śākuntalam. The significance of this principle is to elevate the moral quality of actions above their content. What really matters is the motive inspiring their doing—how actions are done and not what they are.[8]

This doctrine of karma yoga has not only been hailed as the proper interpretation of the *Bhagavadgītā* for our times; it has been hailed as a great, indeed, a grand doctrine not just by the spokespersons of Hinduism but by others as well. The famous French Indologist, Louis Renou, approbates Hinduism in a way which cannot be fully appreciated without understanding the doctrine of svadharma, when he writes:

But ambivalence is characteristic of India: for her, what is the good of killing her cows if she has to lose her soul? A factor in social and psychical equilibrium is found in the notion of *dharma* with its rigorous justice and the 'truth' which it implies (the Indians insist on the attitude of truthfulness as others insist on an 'attitude of consciousness'). An important consequence of this is tolerance, nonviolence considered an active virtue; this is a manner of acting which must be respected—even in the political sphere—*regardless of the attitude of others.* In this perhaps is to be found the most spectacular contribution which India has made to the modern world and the most worthy reply to Marxism and its materialism.[9]

This doctrine, however, has a dark side to it and Hindus have been groping in this darkness for centuries. Stripped to its bone, it is a doctrine of *unilateralism*—of doing one's own duty irrespective of how the other person is behaving. However, if we adopt such an attitude, and it becomes pervasive, we render ourselves vulnerable to manipulation and exploitation at the hands of others. And this is what we have seen happen to communities within Hinduism and to the Hindus as a community. For if we become concerned exclusively with our duty to others, then we tend to pay little attention to their duty towards *us.* It is not considered morally elevating to do so; and it may be morally elevating not to do so but it can, in practical terms, lead, and has led, to gross exploitation. England expected every man to do his duty while it continued collecting its booty. This concern with duty is fine, but the corresponding unconcern with rights—in the name of selfless action—can be highly undesirable. The word yoga alerts us to this danger. The word means not only 'disciple' but also 'acquisition', as in *yogakṣemam vahāmyaham* (IX.22) in the *Gītā* itself. Could it be that the selfless performance of duty is perhaps not inconsistent with an equally selfless assertion of rights in the overall economy of action?

V

The discussion can now be brought to a close. The doctrine of karma is the opposite of fatalism—it was developed not to establish but to prevent such a doctrine. Karma must be understood as vigorous, almost perfectionist action; the doctrine of rebirth, as interpreted for our times, calls upon this very life to be the focus of such dynamic action and the doctrine of karma yoga calls for such dynamic action to be directed towards the assertion of their rights by the Hindus, for even Arjuna was being urged to fight for his rights when the gospel of selfless action was preached to him. This principle applies to Hindus as individuals, as husbands and wives, for instance; to communities within Hinduism, such as Harijans, for instance; and to the Hindus as a community in relation to other communities which dwell alongside them or alongside which they dwell as well.

While I am ready to admit that I do not know how to operationalize this insight, I feel more confident about analysing the implications of its application to another dimension of Hinduism for our times—the dimension of caste. For if now, in modern times, one could go through two or three existential transformations, as it were, on account of increased longevity, literacy and mobility, then clearly birth is no longer a valid index of one's capacity or character. The modern world presents just too many opportunities for the radical transformation of karma.

This point is crucial and therefore may be restated as follows in the traditional idiom. In the traditional caste system birth was used as a basis for determining jāti, and Mahatma Gandhi recommended its use in his own vision of the varṇa system, a vision not lacking in moral grandeur. However, if we examine the point more closely, it could be argued that even in these cases the caste system is based not on birth (or *janma*) but on qualities (or *guṇa*). Once the shock-value of such a seemingly preposterous statement wears off, its main point becomes discernible if not visible. The point is that because it was so difficult to change qualities within a short life—and that is what life was in ancient times as the famous Hobbesian quotation keeps reminding us—one could assume that one basically was what one was born as. The chances of karmic change were so limited; karma was so static that the karmic endowment virtually remained the same from birth to death. To that extent the position that caste may be based on birth *or* worth overstates the case, for karmic inertia secured the rough equation of birth with worth. Hence the acknowledgement of birth as the basis of caste is at bottom an acknowledgement of the assumption of *static* karma rather a disavowal of karma as such as capable of changing one's status even within one lifetime. Such an understanding makes exceptional cases of changes in caste, specially in ancient India, easier to comprehend and to square with the traditional caste system.

It is clear, therefore, that once dynamism in terms of karma is allowed for, the bottom is knocked out of the barrel of the traditional caste system. This, incidentally, also enables us to identify the point of departure of the Gandhian vision of the varṇa system from the traditional caste system, for dynamic karma does *not* knock the bottom out of this barrel. Gandhi advocated vocation based on varṇa not because he believed in static karma but because he was opposed to certain aspects of the modern world such as cut-throat competition, the commodification of labour and the insecurities of unemployment.

Mahatma Gandhi's position on varṇa is as much opposed to the caste system as of those who would allow varṇa to be determined by action rather than birth. Determination of vocation by birth is the kingpin of the Gandhian varṇa system as well, though for a different reason. Unfortunately, it was also the lynchpin of the caste system as such, which Gandhi opposed with his version of the varṇa system. The Gandhian scheme, to my mind, does not quite overcome the guilt by association with birth-ascription which the traditional caste system and the Gandhian varṇa system *share* although they are diametrically opposed in terms of moral implications which follow from this shared basis. Therefore, in this case I am more inclined to agree with those who would that Hinduism changed with the times in this respect, rather than that it tried to change the times to accord with the Gandhian varṇa model. The fine distinction between the Gandhian and traditional models is lost on many; in fact to many it is even invisible.

On the question of caste Radhakrishnan's position changed with the passage of time and this lends some credence to our view that Hinduism too should change with the times in this respect, and that the Gandhian vision of it puts too fine a point on it, a subtlety which ends in futility.[10] In this respect Radhakrishnan consistently inveighed against the caste system, especially after Independence. His brief foreword to T.M.P. Mahadevan's widely used *Outlines of Hinduism*, written on 14 December 1955 is almost equally divided on a positive statement of Hinduism's tolerant spirituality and a negative statement against caste discrimination. It is worth emphasizing that this is a foreword to a book entirely devoted to Hinduism and therefore it would not be unreasonable to assign special significance to the fact that S. Radhakrishnan *chose* to speak of these *two* matters. This fact incidentally also seems to suggest that we may be on the right track in singling them out as having a special bearing on Hinduism for our times. Radhakrishnan applauds the spiritual dimension of Hinduism in the following words:

For the Hindu, the aim of religion is the integration of personality which reconciles the individual to his own nature, his fellowmen and the Supreme Spirit. To realize this goal there are no set paths. Each individual may adopt the method which most appeals to him, and in the atmosphere of Hinduism, even inferior modes of approach get refined. A medieval Indian mystic wrote: 'There may be different kinds of oil in different lamps, the wicks may also be of different kinds, but when they burn, we have the same flame and illumination'.[11]

This is followed by a critique of casteism:

Those who are anchored in spirit suffer for mankind as a whole, regardless of distinctions of caste, class, creed or community. Whereas the truths of religion are eternal, the social forms and institutions are temporary. *They have to be judged by each generation as to their capacity to implement the permanent values.* Some of our institutions have become out of date and require to be modified if not scrapped. In the past religious emotion has attached itself to ugly customs. It has prompted and sanctioned animal sacrifices, obscure rites and oppressive caste regulations. Our sacred literature repudiates discrimination based on birth or *jāti* and emphasises *guṇa* and *karma*. Look at the following verses:

nartako garbha-sambhūto vasiṣṭho-nāma mahā-ṛṣiḥ
tapasā brāhmaṇo jātaḥ, tasmāt jātir na kāraṇam
caṇḍālo garbha sambhūtah śaktir nāma mahā-munih
tapasā brāhmaṇo jātaḥ, tasmat jātir na kāraṇam
śvapāko garbha sambhūtaḥ parāśaro mahā-muniḥ
tapasā brāhmaṇo jātaḥ, tasmat jātir na kāraṇam
matsya-gandhyās tu tanayo vidvān vyāso mahā-muniḥ
tapasā brāhmaṇo jātaḥ, tasmat jātir na kāraṇam.

The *Tirukkural* says: 'All men are born equal. The differences among them are entirely due to occupations' (972).[12]

The statement from the *Tirukkural* that 'all men are born equal' is one of the closest parallels we find in Hinduism of the truth self-evident to Thomas Jefferson that 'all men are created equal', although it is not entirely clear how self-evident it was to him. Evidently he had slaves and even spawned offspring through them, like the *rsis* producing children with the *dāsīs* of yore. By this dubious criterion Jefferson certainly qualifies as a *ṛṣi*, and maybe perhaps by nobler criteria as well.

In 1962 S. Radhakrishnan wrote a preface to another book. This time it was a preface to the monumental five-volume *History of Dharmaśāstra* by P. V. Kane. Two of the six pages, that is, one third of the preface, directly or indirectly addresses the issue of caste.[13] Once again the emphasis is on the undesirability of social discrimination based on birth-ascription and the need for a new social dispensation. It is again pointed out that varṇa is based on action, not birth; that at one time there was only one varṇa, and that conduct alone constitutes the basis of Brahminhood.

The principle of dynamic karma is implied in these statements. If the concept of *dynamic* karma replaces that of *static* karma, then what does it do to the varṇa system as such? Does it blow it apart like dynamite; or is this dynamic dimension of karma capable of transfiguring the varṇa system? An attempt will be made to answer these questions in the next chapter.

Chapter 3

Caste and the Stages of Life in Modern Living

I

Hinduism has often been distinguished from other religions on the basis of two institutions characteristic of it—those of varṇa and *āśrama*, the system of caste and of the stages of life. It is perhaps even more important to recognize that Hinduism has often distinguished *itself* from other religions on this very basis, when such a need arose, and has consciously described itself as *varṇāśrama dharma* or that dharma which is distinguishable from others on the basis of its institutes of varṇa and āśrama. What then are the implications of these social institutions for Hinduism of our times?

II

It may be interesting to begin the discussion of the caste system with the observations of Albiruni, that famous Muslim savant of the eleventh century. He observes about castes at one point:

> Among the Hindus institutions of this kind abound. We Muslims, of course, stand entirely on the other side of the question, considering all men as equal, except in piety; and this is the greatest obstacle which prevents any approach or understanding between Hindus and Muslims.[1]

At another point he observes:

> As **the word of confession,** 'There is no god but God, Muhammad is his prophet,' is the shibboleth of Islam, the Trinity that of Christianity, and the

institute of the Sabbath that of Judaism, so metempsychosis is the shibboleth of the Hindu religion. Therefore he who does not believe in it does not belong to them, and is not reckoned as one of them.[2]

Although Albiruni is prepared to virtually define Hinduism in terms of its belief in reincarnation, he does not seem to forge a link between the doctrine of varṇa and the doctrine of *punarjanma* in accordance with karma, which is the essence of the matter. In the standard Hindu view one's birth in a particular caste is determined by one's karma in a previous life. On account of this oversight, if he is guilty of it, Albiruni fails to note that the Hindus also consider all human beings to be equal 'except in piety' because it is on account of the difference in the degree of piety that they are born in different ('unequal') castes.

Hindu society is divided into commensal and endogamous units called castes, arranged within an overarching fourfold hierarchy of varṇas, one's birth in a particular caste being the result of one's past karma. It is important to recognize that karma is the key to caste, both in the sense of *present* karma or the actions one performs as a member of society (as one's dharma) and in the sense of *past* karma which determined the caste one was born in. Actually *future* karma also enters the picture as the proper performance of one's present karma, that is, one's dharma, ensures rebirth in a higher caste.

This connection of caste and karma—understood in its widest sense—is crucial to a proper understanding of the caste system. This is the common denominator which links otherwise such diverse developments as the caste system itself; the acceptance of the caste system; the rejection of the caste system; the debate within the tradition regarding the caste system; the attempts to reform the caste system, etc.

There is little doubt that a large segment of Hindu society at least willingly if not cheerfully, accepted the caste system. In effect what they were saying was that we accept *past* karma as an adequate explanation of the differences in our present conditions. Those who rejected the caste system were saying in effect that we do not accept the *present* determination of our condition on the basis of karma performed hypothetically in the past.

Our present condition should be determined by our present karma. This provides the clue to the debate within the Hindu tradition whether caste was to be determined by birth or worth; by nature or nurture; by ascription or achievement? Even such a lawgiver as Manu, who has the reputation of being an arch conservative, concedes that a Brāhmaṇa can become a Śūdra in this life if he does not pursue his pious vocation properly (II.168), and actually becomes a Śūdra *in three days* if he sells flesh etc. (X.92) whereas in the *Mahābhārata*, Yudhiṣṭhira says: 'that śūdra who is ever engaged in self-control, truth and righteousness, I regard him a Brahmin' (III.216. 14–15). Hence the ambiguity in the *Gītā*: must Arjuna fight because he is a Kṣatriya or is he to be called a Kṣatriya because he fights?

All the attempts to reform the caste system are rooted in the fact that the link between karma and caste—either in terms of virtuous or vocational conduct—was obscured.[3] It is again a matter of interest that all attempts to abolish or negate the caste system were connected with a new conceptualization of karma. When the inequities of the caste system became too obvious, and its departure from the norms of conduct it was supposed to uphold too blatant, attempts were made (1) either to derive all castes from one caste or reduce them to one caste, (2) or to dispense with the idea of caste altogether, or (3) to spiritualize the caste system.

For example, the *Mahābhārata* says at one point that in the beginning everyone was a Brāhmaṇa: the various castes arose on account of vocational differentiation.[4] Guru Gobind Singh in 1699 took men from all the four castes and made them into Singhas.[5] This 'lionization' of the caste system was really its Kṣatriyization. Mahatma Gandhi declared that as all Hindus were under British servitude they were all Śūdras and should declare their caste in the census as such![6] One can see in each case how the karmic conditions are connected with caste in a novel way.

Those who want to abolish caste altogether appeal to the fact that we are all human beings and all our actions are human actions—*actions* human beings perform in common. Once again caste is connected with action or karma. This is apparent, for instance, in the view which connects the four varṇas with the four *yugas* to draw the following conclusion:

In the golden age only the Brahmins practised austerities, in the second both Brahmins and Kṣatriyas, in the third the three upper classes, and in the fourth all the four classes. In other words, the Hindu scriptures should be thrown open at the present day to all people irrespective of their caste or sex.[7]

The attempt to spiritualize caste consisted of regarding the varṇas as spiritual types which could be related to the various *yogas* or *mārgas* of Hinduism. According to this view the 'four castes represent men of thought, men of action, men of feeling, and others in whom none of these was highly developed'.[8] To spell out the scheme in more detail: the Brāhmaṇa varṇa was meant to practise *jñāna-yoga*; the Kṣatriya varṇa, *karma-yoga*; the Vaiśya varṇa, *bhakti-yoga* and the Śūdra varna, *haṭha-yoga*. Despite this scheme the dialectics seems to have been more effective the other way, for bhakti is known to have mitigated if not eliminated the effect of caste in certain respects.

Nevertheless, even in this scheme it is clear that caste is connected with action, that is, dispositions to various kinds of action—intellectual, executive, affective or physical, even when different castes represented 'members at different stages on the road to self-realization'.[9] If this linkage between caste and karma is accepted then not only does it enable us to understand why the system functioned the way it did in the past, it also enables us to establish the relevance of the caste system to modern living.

Before I make such a daring attempt I would like to lay the ground for it by making three observations.

(1) As I mentioned earlier, in the past, specially prior to the industrial revolution, the level of mobility and literacy was rather restricted. In other words, one's karma could be viewed as fairly static. One was not likely to move away from one's village nor was one very likely to follow a new vocation. It is not that this did not happen, rather these things did not happen on an

appreciable scale, so that *one's birth was a fairly dependable index of one's karma according to the Hindu world-view* under these circumstances. If one was born in a certain situation, life was likely to be more of the same.[10] In these circumstances past karma, in a sense, was much more of a determining variable in life than one's immediate present karma. Modern life is different. Not only is the schoolmaster abroad, many of us go abroad and our lives are no longer confined to the place or even the country of our birth. So I think it is fair to say that present karma should now have preference over past karma, as it preponderates over past karma.

(2) The caste system, as we know it today, is highly if not totally dysfunctional. This statement is not a blanket condemnation or even a criticism of the caste system. All I wish to do is to draw attention to the fact that very few of us follow the vocation of our varṇas! Even within one life we may have changed varṇas. Some of us may have taught for a while at a university and thus functioned as Brāhmaṇas. Prior to that, while paying our way through school we may even have worked in a factory and functioned as a Śūdra. Some left their position in the university and entered the business world— becoming Vaiśyas. And if the countries we were in required a period of compulsory military duty we became Kṣatriyas for that duration. All this is obvious. What is less obvious is that even in classical India one's vocation did not often coincide with one's caste. Consider some of the royal dynasties of ancient India: The Nandas are believed to have been Śūdras; the Śuṅgas were Brāhmaṇas; the Guptas were Vaiśyas and their contemporary, the Vākāṭakas, were again Brāhmaṇas, with whom they entered into a matrimonial alliance; and one seems hard put to identify a Kṣatriya ruling dynasty! The Rāṣṭrakūṭas claimed to be Kṣatriyas of lunar descent.

(3) The caste system is not the first Hindu institution to become dysfunctional. At one time Hinduism was dominated by sacrificial rituals in which live animals were sacrificed. This

is hardly the case today—in fact sacrificial ritual of that kind went out of vogue centuries ago. It was on its way out once the Upaniṣads started gaining in importance. But Hinduism, with its instinct for conservation does not abandon anything outright—it allegorizes or internalizes it. In the Upaniṣads spiritual exercises performed mentally were said to be as potent as sacrifices performed externally. In fact, once an aspect of Hinduism becomes dysfunctional, it becomes ripe for reinterpretation.

It is precisely this which I now intend to discuss. Many of us are aware of the account of the origin of the varṇas as described in the Puruṣasūkta of the *Ṛg Veda*. Out of the mouth of the cosmic being emerged the Brāhmaṇa; out of his arms the Kṣatriya; out of his thighs the Vaiśya and out of his feet the Śūdra. Such distinctions may have been appropriate for an age when literacy was low and the main avenue for the acquisition of professional expertise was one's family. But now, given the aim of universal literacy and the fact of global mobility, I suggest that, for our times, we consider all the four varṇas as contained in all of us and call this the doctrine of *sārvavārṇikatā*. The idea is that *all* the varṇas are contained in *every* individual from now on instead of every individual being comprised within only one of the varṇas. But this is not meant as a glib rationalization. It imposes a fourfold obligation on every Hindu:

(1) As a Brāhmaṇa every Hindu must have minimal familiarity with the Hindu scriptures and rituals;

(2) As a Kṣatriya every Hindu must undergo compulsory military training as well as experience political empowerment by participating in the political process;[11]

(3) As a Vaiśya every Hindu must train for a profession, that is, undergo required vocational preparation and pursue a vocation; and

(4) As a Śūdra every Hindu must perform some form of manual labour or service.

III

Like the varṇas the āśrama system is also a characteristic feature of Hinduism. Kālidāsa, the famous Sanskrit poet, composed an epic called the *Raghuvaṁśa* to glorify the Sūryavaṁśī rulers or kings who claimed descent from the sun in terms of Hindu mythology. In one verse therein he states that members of this royal line (1) spent their childhood in acquiring knowledge; (2) their youth in savouring the pleasures of life; (3) their later life in living like anchorites and (4) finally ended their life through the practise of yoga. Herein we find a poetic description of the stages of life: (1) of *Brahmacarya* or life as a celibate student until one turned twenty-five; (2) of *Gṛhastha* or the life of a householder until one reached the age of fifty; (3) of *Vānaprastha* or the life of retirement in a hermitage and (4) *Sannyāsa* or the life of a wandering ascetic till one passed on.

In order to understand the inner logic of these stages of life one must once again identify the key concept in terms of which it is operating. In the case of the caste system or *varṇavyavasthā* it turned out to be karma. In the case of the *āśramavyavasthā* the key terms are *pravṛtti* and *nivṛtti* or engagement in and disengagement from worldly life. If we look at the four stages of life closely, they are really amplifications of two stages of life—a life of active engagement in the world till the age of fifty, and a life of gradual disengagement from life in the world until its abandonment towards the end. In this sense the key stages then are gṛhastha and sannyāsa. Brahmacarya is a preparation *ultimately* perhaps for both, but *proximately* for gṛhastha and retirement to the hermitage or vānaprastha is quite clearly a preparation for final renunciation.

Just as in relation to varṇa one of the issues all along had been whether it should be based on past-life karma or present-life karma, the central issue in relation to āśrama has been whether pravṛtti and nivṛtti should be practised successively or simultaneously. And just as in the case of varṇa the classical consensus had been in favour of past-life karma, in the case of āśrama the classical consensus had been in favour of a synthesis through succession: a life of worldly engagement followed by a life of disengagement from the world. And just as in the case of the varṇa system, in the context of modern living, I proposed a shift to present-life karma and an internalization of the four varṇas, I suggest the simultaneous pursuit of pravṛtti and nivṛtti and the 'diurnalization' of the four āśramas.

The concept of the simultaneous pursuit of pravṛtti and nivṛtti has already been elaborated in the *Bhagavadgītā*. It is hazardous to claim to have deciphered the meaning of so popular, protean and pregnant a text but I am inclined to believe that the *Bhagavadgītā* favours a present-life karma view of karma and perhaps even more indisputably a 'renunciation in action' or nivṛtti in pravṛtti view of life. Once attachment and detachment are identified not in terms of actual external acts but rather with the *attitude* with which they are performed, the results of renunciation need not be achieved by locomotion, i.e. by leaving the world, they can be achieved by meditation i.e. by detached living within the world.

This being the case, in a modern world characterized by flexitime, annual vacations and so on, it becomes possible to suggest that the four stages of life could be compressed within the confines of a day. This minisculization is what I referred to as diurnalization of the āśramas as a counterpart to the interiorization of the varṇas. The suggestion here is to treat each day as encapsulating a lifetime. Thus in the morning one is in the stage of brahmacarya—one spends time in matutinal study of the scriptures and in morning devotion; the forenoon and afternoon are spent in as a gṛhastha, as a householder and in earning a livelihood to run the house. In the evening one spends some time in quite contemplation with one's wife, an activity which answers to vānaprastha. (In actual life one is more likely to watch TV and instead become a *TV Prastha*!) Finally, before retiring for the night, one meditates on the highest truth, divesting oneself completely of the distractions of daily life. At first sight the idea of becoming a sannyāsī at night might sound rather strange. The idea of a daytime gṛhastha and a nocturnal sannyāsī will appear less fanciful if we recognize that all the four āśramas are based on the opposition as well apposition of pravṛtti and nivṛtti: that is to say, engagement in the world which typically occurs during the day and withdrawal from such activities, which typically takes place at night. One renounces all the actions of the day at night. Viṣṇu's *yoganidrā* or mystic slumber during the intervals between the ages provides both the pattern and the paradigm in this case and serves to reinforce our suggestion and lends it credence. The attempt to run the day on the analogy of a life is not as far-fetched as it might appear at first sight. Apart from the secular wisdom of living one day at a time, within the Hindu tradition sleep has been described as daily death (*dainandinaṁ maraṇam*)!

In as much as the twin doctrines of varṇa and āśrama go hand in hand, it may be worth noting, as P. V. Kane has pointed out, that 'the theory of varṇa dealt with man as a member of the aryan society' while the 'theory of the āśramas addressed itself to the individual'.[12] In these terms our reinterpretation of these doctrines involves an introversion: in the case of the varṇas the focus of the doctrine has been shifted from the social to the individual dimension and in the case of the āśrama from the outer to the inner human being. There also exists the extreme etymological option of defining varṇa in terms of the colour of one's karma as white or black as in the *Yogasūtras* (IV.7) and āśrama as any stage, even a stage 'in which one exerts oneself', for those who would like to attenuate these threads in the fabric of Hinduism even further. This however is a development which the Hindu religious tradition has, so far, as far as possible tried to evade.

Many scholars have drawn attention to the fact that more than varṇa it is the concept of jāti which represents the social reality of Hindu and even Indian life more accurately, so much so that some scholars have even gone to the extent of describing the Hindu social reality exclusively in terms of jātis. There is much truth in this view, especially as even social units fully conscious of their varṇa status act in accordance with their jāti. For instance, although in theory a Brahmin family in UP can interdine and intermarry with a Brahmin family in Kerala or a Kṣatriya family from the Punjab with one in Āndhra, typically this does not happen, leading M. Duncan M. Derrett to comment that in these matters the Hindus have been more orthodox than their scriptures.[13] How then is the foregoing analysis affected by this circumstance?

The varṇa system is essentially vertical, while the jāti system is essentially horizontal. That is to say, jātis belong to or are connected with one of the four varṇas although they might dispute their relative ranking within it. Thus, theoretically, the analysis carried out above does not present any serious obstacle to the discussion carried out earlier, as each jāti is connected to a varṇa and is brought, through this connection, within the ambit of the varṇa and hence within the range of our earlier discussion, which can thus be said to embrace the entire gamut of varṇa and jāti in theory.

In practice, however, a difficulty may arise. Social self-consciousness may be tied to one's jāti identity to the point of obliviousness and even denial of the larger category of varṇa, and to that extent the application of our analysis of jāti as subsumed within varṇa may not correspond to field reality. The problem in such cases is perhaps resolved by the universalization of jāti—a sentiment common to Vedic and Puranic literature—that all human beings belong to one jāti or race, namely the human.

IV

At this point a very different perspective could be brought tobear on the whole question. Some have wondered whether we need to worry about this issue at all, especially from the standpoint of economic theory. It could be suggested that the institutions of varṇa and āśrama are not *states* which inherently characterize social and individual life, but *stages* in the process of economic evolution which are destined to be dissolved in due course by the solvents of economic progress. This is a point of view which both the Capitalist and Communist perspectives on life share in common to a degree.

According to the Capitalist vision, as the industrial revolution established itself in India, to the accompaniment of functional differentiation, occupational mobility and rapid industrialization, the pre-industrial socio-economic structure, which is what the varṇāśrama really is in a religious guise according to this view, would automatically disappear and religion would become an entirely private affair, as secularization proceeded to mould society in its own shape. The forces of capitalism would thus ensure the demise of the varṇāśrama system, which would slip out of sight unmourned, like the past year on New Year's eve. Hence there is no need to besiege the citadel philosophically or theologically as we have done, for it is destined to crumble anyway.

According to the Communist vision there was even less need for intervention. Religion itself represented an ideational superstructure, closely related to the disposition of the means of production and the distribution of that production in society. As soon as these changed, the superstructure would collapse and be succeeded by science. According to a less radical view the superstructure would itself get modified beyond recognition, as its economic basis changed. Moreover, ideologically, the Marxist vision saw society divided horizontally between the bourgeoisie and the proletariat rather than into varṇas and the communists did not visualize human life passing through stages, other than the biological.

If we add to this the fact that in the early years of Independence a mixed economy was espoused—a mix of the capitalist and communist systems—then the speedy dissolution of the varṇāśrama system seemed even more of a foregone conclusion, for now *two* forces were at work to produce the same outcome. Its dissolution was to be a revolution achieved without firing a shot—the natural and welcome outcome of impersonal economic forces operating under a mixed economy, with the logic of capitalism and communism reinforcing each other in possessing a common fatalism regarding the future of religious institutions and perhaps religion itself.

Had the vision unfolded as it has been described above, this chapter would not have been necessary; no more than a chapter is required to spell out how progressively the disabilities of women and Śūdras in relation to studying the Vedas were removed in modern Hinduism. The printing press took care of that, and modern sanitation could similarly take care of untouchability. It might still well be the case but events have shown that economic determinism, however progressive, has proved less of a magic wand; rather it has turned out to be the maestro's wand which might—if not handled carefully—produce much social cacophony. In this respect Max Weber, it seems, has proved closer to the mark than Karl Marx. In India the stirrings of religious nationalism were first felt by its economically better-off group, the Sikhs, which on Marxist assumptions should have moved *away* from religion more swiftly than its other less prosperous Indian counterparts. India, more prosperous now than in 1947, is also today religiously at least equally if not more self-conscious than it was in 1947 and is certainly more caste-conscious now than it was then. Culture has turned out to be more intransigent to economic forces than the founding fathers of India bargained for. The events of the past half century have clearly demonstrated the limited ability of secular economic forces to alter religious ideas and institutions, not only in India but in the world at large.

The recent rise of fundamentalism the world over has taken secularists by surprise. The secularists saw religiosity as declining steadily until it disappeared. This was the prevailing expectation in the 1960s. It seems, however, as if the often-quoted statement about religion being the opium of the people came to exercise an opiate influence on the scholars who trusted and cited it. While they were lulled into a false sense of security under its influence in the eventual disappearance of religion, religion emerged unexpectedly as a major force in world politics in the 1980s. The 1980s witnessed the turning of the intellectual tables and the secular theory of religion, one might say, almost gave way to a religious theory of secularism. It came to be argued that religion represents an anthropological need, which is universal but not constant (like hunger). To think that religion has disappeared just because society is passing through a secular phase is like imagining that one will never need food because one is not hungry at the present moment. Moreover, religion and society interact in complex ways. Even if it is conceded that social phenomena are not independent of secular or economic reality, it does not mean that they can be reduced to it. Two simple examples may be cited to illustrate this point. Economic development was supposed to loosen the bonds of caste but the elaborate reservations for Scheduled Castes and Tribes and Other Backward Classes support the view that even if the forces which produce the pie may turn a blind eye to caste, the way the pie is divided up in society is at least affected by it. Moreover, individual examples like that of Dr B. R. Ambedkar, who has been hailed as the father of the Indian Constitution, indicate that social ideas can be forces in and of themselves. Although he was better educated than many Brahmins and even knew Sanskrit, it has been alleged that there was still a residual reluctance on the part of many to accept him as an equal on account of his untouchable origins. Thus, while secular developments may help, it remains a moot point whether one can do without an ideological reorientation of the tradition in these matters to achieve the intended ameliorative result. This point is pursued further in the next section.[14]

V

Hence the fact that Hinduism or Hindu dharma is still ideologically equated with varṇāśrama dharma, even if the principle is honoured more in its breach than in actual practice, still remains to be tackled. The Hindus subscribe to the varṇāśrama system in theory but not in practice. M. Hiriyanna has drawn attention to a similar phenomenon in the history of Hindu philosophy. He writes, after pointing out that the two schools of Hindu thought—the Pūrvamimāṁsā and the Uttara-mimāṁsā—are based on Vedic revelation:

> The name 'mīmāṁsā,' given to these systems, means systematic investigation, and shows the important place assigned to reflection (*vicāra*) in India even in the doctrines based upon revelation. The ultimate appeal in them may not be to reason: but, at the same time, they do not signify a blind reliance on untested and unsupported authority. *They may consequently be taken as rationalistic in practice, though not in theory.*[15]

Perhaps the discrepancy between theory and practice in the present case can, at least in part, be traced to the vigorous opposition the caste system also has had to face in Hinduism both from within and without and such opposition has again produced a fortunate result. Lest it be considered that I may have overestimated the potential of the danger of the virulence of the caste system as a cellular mechanism gone mad, let me recount Albiruni's account of the Vāmanāvatāra or the incarnation of Viṣṇu as a dwarf. He writes, on the basis of the text before him, that Viṣṇu sent Bali to the nether world because Bali had the temerity to abolish caste distinctions. Albiruni then proceeds to quote Narāyaṇa:

> I do that to him only for this purpose that the equality between men, which he desires to realise, shall be done away with, that men shall be different in their conditions of life, and that on this difference the order of the world is to be based; further, that people shall turn away from *his* worship and worship *me* and believe in *me*. The mutual assistance of civilised people presupposes a certain difference among them, in consequence of which the one requires the other. According to the same principle, God has created the world as containing many differences in itself. So the single countries differ from each other, one being cold, the other warm; one having good soil, water, and air, the other having bitter salt soil, dirty and bad smelling water, and unhealthy air. There are still more differences of this kind; in some cases advantages of all kinds being numerous, in others few. In some parts there are periodically returning physical disasters; in others they are entirely unknown. All these things induce civilised people carefully to select the places where they want to build towns.
>
> That which makes people do these things is usage and custom. However, religious commands are much more powerful, and influence much more the nature of man than usages and customs. The bases of the latter are investigated, explored, and accordingly either kept or abandoned, whilst the bases of

the religious commands are left as they are, not inquired into, adhered to by the majority simply on *trust.* They do not argue over them, as the inhabitants of some sterile region do not argue over it, since they are born in it and do not know anything else, for they love the country as their fatherland, and find it difficult to leave it. If, now, besides physical differences, the countries differ from each other also in law and religion, there is so much attachment to it in the hearts of those who live in them that it can never be rooted out.[16]

I have quoted the passage at some length despite the fact that it is tedious in places, because it contains a vital clue which I will develop at length later. The clue is provided by the juxtaposition of the first and the last sentence in the passage. The first sentence reads:

I do that to him only for this purpose that the equality between men, which he desires to realise, shall be done away with, that men shall be different in their conditions of life, and that on this difference the order of the world is to be based;...

That is to say: caste distinctions are natural and sustain the world order. The last sentence reads:

If, now, besides physical differences, the countries differ from each other also in law and religion, there is so much attachment to it in the hearts of those who live in them that it can never be rooted out.

That is to say: religious differences are natural and ineradicable. Thus distinctions of *caste* and distinctions of *religion* are on par: it is as heinous to change one's religion as one's caste, or vice versa.

VI

The case of Bali and the incarnation of Viṣṇu as Vāmana is particularly interesting from another point of view, as indicating the window of egalitarianism which existed even within the four walls of the varṇas. To identify this window of opportunity one needs to refer back to the account as found in Albiruni and perhaps even beyond. Albiruni explicitly states that Bali 'on having heard from his mother that the time of his father had been much better than *his* time, since it was nearer the *kṛita-yuga,* when people enjoyed more profound bliss, and did not know any fatigue, he became ambitious and desirous of vying with his father' and almost succeeded.[17]

The point to note is that Bali wanted to revive the Sat Yuga. Now this ideal state of affairs in the Sat Yuga is visualized in four ways in Hindu myths: (1) that in this age all the four varṇas functioned harmoniously; (2) that this age was predominantly Brahmin or (3) that in this age only Brahmins existed; namely that there was only one varṇa which is in a sense the same as having no varṇa or that (4) no varṇas existed at all per se. In the various accounts of Bali's restoration of Sat Yuga each of these implications can be traced.[18] The general trend, however, is clear in terms of *vārṇika* harmony achieved through any of these four interpretations.

The idea that the golden age is characterized by the attenuation if not elimination of caste distinctions is further confirmed by the festival of Balipratipadā already described by Albiruni.[19] It is believed that on this day Bali is allowed to return to his kingdom to rule for one day. The significance of the reversal of the norms of classical Hinduism implied in this should not be lost sight of. One may also recall here 'a tie between Bali and Kerala's Oṇam Festival, and a portrayal of Bali's rule as a golden age in Kerala's past'.[20]

The general move away from any sense of caste discrimination and caste conflict towards virtual caste elimination is characteristic of the cycles of Bali stories and it is a point of at least equal if not greater interest that this trend sometimes culminates in what in modern parlance is called egalitarianism. The *Mahābalicaritam* specifically states that when 'Mahābali was king all men were equal'.[21] This is, of course, contrary, or at least different, from the more usual view of the social order found in Hinduism and hence constitutes a window of vulnerability in its generally hierarchical orientation.

It is thus a point not devoid of interest that the same word dharma is used both for caste duty and for religion in our languages of India today and that the Hindus might apply the *Gītā's* admonition of not abandoning one's dharma as carrying this double-barrelled blast against changing either. This point will be examined in greater detail later.

VII

While elaborating on the reformulations of the doctrines of varṇa and āśrama which I discussed earlier, I would specially like to draw attention to three points in this respect.

(1) The manner in which I have tried to present the new understanding of varṇa and āśrama contains not one but two tiers of understanding; it contains two dimensions, an internal or interior one and an external or exterior one. Alternatively, they might also be considered as individual and social one. The idea that, on the pattern of the primeval person, all the four varṇas are contained within oneself, just as all the limbs representing them are, is an internalized or interiorized understanding of the four varṇas. All the varṇas converge and merge in the individual, making him or her accountable in terms of all—at the most basic level. Socially, however, it is clear that individuals will belong to different vocations irrespective of birth, for by birth, according to my analysis, one has *already been implicated inherently* into all the four varṇas. My view differs from that of Mahatma Gandhi in this respect, which only shows my veneration for him, for in my Hinduism to differ from your hero is to truly revere him; it means that you have travelled further from him in the direction in which he pointed. Reverting to the social dimension of varṇa, it is the natural implication of the above view that one's exterior varṇa will change with change of vocation, as seems to be the current practice in Bali, the Hindu outpost in Indonesia. 'In Bali varṇa is simply occupation. A businessman is a vaiśya, a teacher a Brahmin, an employee a śūdra and so on. No inferior or superior status is attached, and if one switches profession—say from teacher to shopkeeper—one changes caste from Brahmin to vaiśya'.[22] Was this the case in ancient India too at some time, for in the *Kathāsaritsāgara* a father asks his daughter: 'To which of the four varṇas would you like your husband to belong?'[23]

This means that the concept of svadharma must now be interpreted on its own, independently of the scaffolding provided by the varṇa system, though it could well be that the callings which various individuals pursue could still be capable of being classified according to the traditional varṇa categories in a social or external sense. Any such connection, however, will now be casual rather than causal, or better still, coincidental rather than consequential. Moreover, since one's own dharma is now self-defined, it overcomes the shadow side of niṣkāma karma yoga identified earlier. Several positive ends are thus simultaneously achieved at a single stroke.

Similarly with the āśramas. At the internal, interior or individual level the underlying concept implies nivṛtti or inner detachment in pravṛtti or external action. At the external level two possibilities arise. I suggested earlier how all the four stages could be compressed in a day. To those, however, for whom such compression smacks of distortion, the periodization could cover longer spans of time, till in the end perhaps spending time in an actual āśrama or retreat would itself constitute a stage of life traversed not during the course of a day but a year. The important point here, unlike in the case of varṇa, is the *flexibility not in terms of categories but of the categories themselves.* It is well known, for instance, that originally each of the four āśramas may have signified distinct life styles pursued throughout life, instead of each representing a phase of life. Indeed, thinking about the āśramas has always been characterized by a certain fluidity in Hinduism as distinguished from the doctrine of the four varṇas. P. V. Kane notes that 'with reference to the four āśramas, there are three different points of view (pakṣas) viz *samuccaya* (orderly co-ordination), *vikalpa* (option) and *bādha* (annulment or contradiction)'.[24] The samuccaya view of orderly co-ordination involves resorting to the four āśramas in that order, while leapfrogging from brahmacarya to sannyāsa, as in the case of people like Śaṅkarācārya, represents an illustration of vikalpa. The view which gives pre-eminence to gṛhasthāśrama as the āśrama par excellence is known as bādha, as it debars the exercise of other options. An attempt is also made to reconcile these divergent views in typical Hindu fashion.[25]

(2) The suggestions I have made regarding reinterpreting the traditional concepts of varṇa and āśrama along radical lines are not really as radical as they seem, for if we take the word radical

in its 'radical' sense, namely as pertaining to roots, they are merely another flowering or fruit of the root concepts or perhaps metaphors which they embody. I have merely marched, a little further perhaps, on the tracks left by seers of old. Already the *Śvetāśvatara Upaniṣad*, for instance, hints at a kind of life which does not conform to the āśramas as such, for the wise Śvetāśvatara is stated therein as discoursing on Brahman to the *atyāśramī(s)* (VI.22). The expression is usually taken to represent ascetics of the most advanced stage but is capable of yielding other senses as well.[26] The same Upaniṣad uses the word varṇa but steers clear of the four varṇas in a famous verse (IV.2):

> He who is one, without any colour (*avarṇo*), by the manifold exercise of his power distributes many colours (*varṇān*) in his hidden purpose . . .[27]

(3) I must acknowledge my debt to the *Bhagavadgītā* in making such suggestions as I have made, while making it clear at the same time that while in some ways I have gone beyond the *Gītā*, in other ways I haven't gone far enough. It is well known that the doctrine on which I have based my reinterpretation of the āśramas is central to our modern understanding of the *Bhagavadgītā*, with its emphasis of renunciation *in* action rather than renunciation *of* action, despite the fact that 'there is not much reference in the [*Gītā*] to āśrama-dharma, the twin companion of Varṇa-Dharma'.[28]

The case of its influence on the reformulation of the doctrine of the varṇa is more complex. In the eighteenth chapter the *Bhagavadgītā* connects the four varṇas with the guṇas (XVIII.41). Although in the text itself the word guṇa alone appears, commentators unanimously explain the word as referring to the three guṇas of *sattva*, *rajas* and *tamas*.[29] The striking fact here is that in the immediately preceding verse the text asserts (XVIII.40) that no creature whatsoever exists, whether on the earth or in the sky or among the gods who does not possess these *three* guṇas. This means that no human being exists who does not contain these three guṇas and by extension all the four varṇas, with which these guṇas are inescapably connected *within himself or herself.* This kind of equation suits my argument well. I must clarify, however, that although I am happy to say so with the *Gītā*, if it can be made to say it, I do not say what I say because of it.

In one crucial respect, nevertheless, I stop short of the *Gītā*. In the sixty-sixth verse of the last chapter of the *Gītā*, which in the Viśiṣṭādvaita tradition is regarded as the *carama śloka*—the ultimate verse of the *Gītā*—Kṛṣṇa asks Arjuna to forsake all dharmas (sarvadharmān) and cleave to Kṛṣṇa alone. Now all means all and Kṛṣṇa is All-in-All. As All-in-all Kṛṣṇa is asking Arjuna to forsake all dharmas, these must include the varṇa and āśrama dharmas as well. I sometimes think that the full import of this verse has, strangely enough, been overlooked perhaps because it is so drastic. Kṛṣṇa is ultimately asking Arjuna to give up all dharmas—including the varṇa and āśrama dharmas—and seek refuge in Him alone. I have not gone that far in my reinterpretation of the doctrines of varṇa and āśrama; I have not suggested their abandonment, only their reinterpretation. After all, I am not God, who can simultaneously, with the abandonment of all dharmas also offer release from all sins. So I have had to stop short.

Chapter 4

Hindu Tolerance

I

The pluralistic nature of Hinduism is well known. In discussing the sources of dharma, different understandings of it can be identified; with respect to karma and rebirth, again a wide range of views can be adduced. In the discussion of the doctrines of varṇa and āśrama one once again encounters a whole battery of views. And yet, in saying all this if one is guilty of anything, it is of understatement rather than of overstatement. But does this mean that Hinduism does not draw the line anywhere? It is obvious that it does possess some sense of self-definition even if it is vis-à-vis others, otherwise we would not be able to discourse about it. It obviously has borders, but these borders are indefinitely extensible; it is not that it has no demarcating lines, rather that these lines can be redrawn.

In order to understand Hindu tolerance one must begin by appreciating the nature of Hindu universalism. This universalism is not a blanket universalism. If one stands beside a vast lake and sees the endless sky reflected in the waters of the lake completely and thoroughly, then for a moment one doesn't know the sky from the lake. A simple way of reverting to the less sublime reality of the world is to throw a pebble in the water; the expanding concentric circles of the ripples formed on the water will remind us of where we stand. They will also go on spreading in ever-widening circles until they subside and the pristine purity of the waters of the lake is restored. Hindu universalism is more like the vastness of a vast body of water than that of the blue sky. It is dynamic. Once disturbed, it spreads out like ripples to reach as far as it can and embrace as much as it can. This disturbance arises when its consciousness of universalism is challenged.

Hinduism is conscious of its universalism because it considers consciousness to be the most universal dimension of existence. It arrived at this conclusion, however, by stages in Vedic times. By retaining its stadial character but replacing them by modern analogues we may be able to probe the emergence of this belief in the universalism of consciousness which lies at the root of its consciousness of universalism, and hence its tolerance.

Let us begin with theistic consciousness or the awareness of God. Let us then ask of it the penetrating question: Which is more universal—theistic consciousness or moral consciousness? One may not believe in God, but everyone possesses a sense of right and wrong. We may not all agree on the exact content of what constitutes right and wrong, but all of us, without exception, possess a sense of right and wrong. Or as Mahatma Gandhi puts it: denial of God we have known, denial of truth we have not. This realization led him to reverse his famous equation 'God is Truth' into 'Truth is God'.

Moving a step further, one can ask an even more penetrating question: which is more universal, moral consciousness or aesthetic consciousness? The ability of music to soothe the savage breast is well known. Even the most rudimentary moralist responds to the overtures of a dance and even a criminal's body begins to keep time with the steady beat of a drum. Arguably then, aesthetic consciousness is more universal than moral consciousness. The charge of amoralism levelled against Zen Buddhism, though it can still not be condoned, can at least now be understood. Zen assimilates itself to art rather than to conventional morality perhaps because the former is more universal.

We are deep in the woods but there is scope to delve even deeper by asking yet another and even more penetrating question:

which is more universal, aesthetic awareness or sexual awareness? Not everyone consummates a marriage with consummate skill; sexual physical awareness is more universal than artistic or aesthetic awareness. This realization may help us understand Tantra as a dimension of Hinduism more sympathetically. Be that as it may, one more question remains to be asked. We discovered successively that moral consciousness was more universal than theistic consciousness, that aesthetic consciousness was more universal than moral consciousness, that sexual or physical consciousness was more universal than aesthetic consciousness. Now the question arises: which is more universal, sexual consciousness or self-consciousness; or, to rephrase the question, physical consciousness or mental consciousness.

It thus emerges that consciousness, which by its very nature is immaterial, is the most universal entity of all. It is for this reason that among the religions of the world, while other religions have tended to centre themselves on God or morality or beauty, or sensuality, Hinduism has centred itself on consciousness itself. By centring itself on the most universal entity of all, it now claims to be the most universal entity among them all.

In actual relationship this celebration of the universal finds its expression within Hinduism as tolerance, as we descend from the stratosphere of the ideal into the atmosphere of the actual. Much has been written about Hindu tolerance; but this pervasive acceptance of tolerance and of the idea that Hinduism is tolerant has had one unfortunate consequence. Familiarity with a concept sometimes inclines us to take it for granted; familiarity breeds the illusion of knowledge through sheer familiarity.

II

I shall now examine this concept of tolerance critically, first, by defining what tolerance means and does *not* mean; second, by analysing the consequences the practice of tolerance has had for Hinduism; third, by pointing out the limits of tolerance; and finally, by offering my own suggestion regarding the exercise of tolerance in our own times.

Tolerance has been defined as 'a permissive or liberal attitude towards beliefs and practices differing from or conflicting with one's own' (*Webster's Third International Dictionary*, p. 2405). As with the case of Hinduism, so also with Hindu tolerance, it is best to proceed by the negative way of indicating what Hindu tolerance does not mean.

(1) In Hinduism, tolerance does *not* mean approval. Once when Mahatma Gandhi was criticized for criticizing Christianity while claiming to be tolerant, he pointed out that tolerance should not be confused with approval. In addition to Mahatma Gandhi's willingness to criticize other religions while claiming to, and I would maintain, remaining tolerant, consider the following facts: Hinduism has had a vigorous tradition of debate not only with other religions and philosophies of Indian origin such as Buddhism, Jainism and Hindu materialism but also, subsequently, with Islam and Christianity; within Hinduism certain practices both Vedic, such as that of animal sacrifices and post-Vedic, such as that of suttee, have been repeatedly criticized. Thus, tolerance should not be confused with approval. What it does imply is the recognition of the distinction between coercion and criticism. Coercion is not consistent with tolerance; criticism is, so is persuasion. One should distinguish between coercion at one extreme and indulgence on the other; and tolerance should not be confused with indulgence.

(2) Tolerance does *not* mean the absence of conflict but represents an attitude towards it both during the conflict and after it. Hinduism believes in truth, goodness and justice not in the sense that error and evil are not present but that they are not ultimate or final. Similarly, Hindu tolerance does not represent a naive faith in the absence of conflict but a robust confidence in the overcoming of it. Once such a conflict is overcome, Hindu tolerance represents magnanimity rather than vindictiveness in victory. The establishment of Vedic rule in the Punjab and early Hebrew rule in Canaan provide a useful contrast here. In both

the cases military defeat of one's enemies was involved—of the *Dāsas* and *Dasyus* in the *Ṛg Veda* and the Canaanites in the Hebrew Bible. But once this victory was achieved, the deities of the defeated peoples were accepted by the Vedic Hindus on the dictum that 'The real is one, sages call is variously' (*Ṛg Veda* I.164.46). On the other hand, the early Hebrews were of the view that their God Yahweh is a 'jealous God' who declared 'Thou shalt have no other Gods but me' (Exodus 20:3) and local cults were crushed. In order to be fair to Judaism it must be added that this attitude is not characteristic of post-biblical Judaism. Its later attitudes are similar to those found within Hinduism.

(3) Tolerance does *not* mean absence of preference. As we all know, Hindus have remarkable freedom in choosing their *iṣṭa-devatā* or the deity chosen for the sake of personal devotion, whether it be Viṣṇu, or any of his incarnations or Śiva, or any member of their families, etc. But while it gives to everyone the right to choose for oneself, it does not give one the right to reject someone else's choice. If I worship Rāma I am free to consider Rāma as my own chosen deity and I may insist that for me subjectively, Rama is the only deity; but this does not give me the right to deny others the choice of their own. In other words, what tolerance implies is not an absence of preference but rather an absence of exclusion.

(4) Tolerance does *not* always means an achievement thereof and may remain an aspiration; it may sometimes be properly understood as an attitude rather than as an accomplishment. The issue of tolerance often involves two parties. The Hindu position, that in religious matters 'You are OK; I am OK' may not be accepted by the other party which might insist 'I am OK; you are not OK'. In such a situation Hindu tolerance implies the view that perhaps the other party can be brought around to share a mutually acceptable platform. It represents the attitude which seeks unity in diversity; harmony in discord; the universal in the particular; the common in the different; the integrative over the disruptive—but this may not always be achieved.

(5) Tolerance is *not* absolute but relative. Even in Hindu India there have been occasional outbursts of fanaticism against Buddhism and Jainism, and within Hinduism sometimes one sect has been intolerant of another. But on the whole there is little doubt that Hinduism has been far more tolerant when compared with the Semitic religious tradition, specially as represented by Christianity and Islam.

(6) Tolerance does *not* mean that a religion may not be missionary. Buddhism is a striking example of a tolerant but missionary religion. Hinduism too has been missionary, but tolerance of missionary activity does mean that Hinduism does *not* tolerate certain questionable means of missionary activity, such as use of force, fraud or inducement.

(7) Tolerance is not just an attitude which distinguishes the attitude of Hinduism towards *other* religions. It is also an attitude which is characteristically found within Hinduism as well. Abbé Dubois, a French cleric who visited south India in the eighteenth century, was surprised to find that sectarian differences did not complicate Hindu married life. He wrote:

> In some parts a remarkable peculiarity is to be observed in reference to these two sects. Sometimes the husband is a Vishnavite and bears the **namam** on his forehead, while the wife is a follower of Siva and wears the **lingam.** The former eats meat, but the latter may not touch it. This divergency of religious opinion, however, in no way destroys the peace of the household. Each observes the practices of his or her own particular creed, and worships his or her god in the way that seems best, without any interference from the other.[1]

In other words, in relation to Hinduism, tolerance is both an inter-religious and an intra-religious phenomenon. In fact, it can even be argued that its tolerant attitude towards other religions is an extrapolation of this attitude within it.

(8) Tolerance is *not* to be confused with defeat or docility or folly, no more than we can allow someone to take away our belongings on the ground that we are tolerant. Tolerance must be voluntary; enforced tolerance under duress is not tolerance. When the Zoroastrians came to India and were willingly

allowed to settle down, that constituted tolerance. But, when foreign rulers occupied the throne of Delhi, their presence in India did not represent Hindu religious tolerance, it represented defeat.

(9) Tolerance is *not* static. As norms change, so does tolerance. For instance, the Upaniṣads, along with what are regarded as great spiritual insights, also refer to trial by ordeal. At that time the practice was considered acceptable but was replaced by trial by courts of law and in due course was no longer considered tolerable.

(10) Hindu tolerance does *not* mean that religiously defined communities may not come into conflict on non-religious grounds; they may, for instance, come into conflict on political grounds. Hindu tolerance means that for a Hindu the cause of conflict will not be religious, i.e. the other person does not have to be fought with because he or she is not a Hindu. Hindu tolerance means that the source of conflict between Hindus and non-Hindus will not be on grounds that the religious beliefs and practices of other persons are different from those of the Hindus; but it could well take place on the ground that *Hindu beliefs and practices are different from those of others.*

III

One must now also recognize that just as dogmatism is a sign of intolerance; indiscriminate tolerance can be a sign of mental laziness or moral fecklessness. In other words, tolerance has its limits. They may briefly be summed up as follows.

Moral Limits: Certain doctrines or practices may be so repugnant or become so repugnant that their tolerance may be neither desirable nor practical. For instance, the practice of worshipping deities by offering one's children in sacrifice (also found in the Bible) may not be tolerated, nor one which involves suicide, such as suttee. Similarly, with the growth in moral consciousness what was tolerable at one time may become intolerable in due course. Untouchability is a recent example; levirate an ancient one.

Practical Limits: Total absence of restraint in the form of unqualified tolerance may render social existence impossible. For instance, will one tolerate a salesperson who wants to observe the vow of silence during business hours? At a more general level, something has to hold the diverse beliefs and practices together. It is in this sense that Vedic authority, the sanctity of the cow, caste rules, etc. make sense. In the intellectual arena there is a nominal acceptance of Vedic authority; but Hinduism is not merely a philosophy but a religion as well. Hence, in terms of practice the cow is sacred—but outcastes eat beef. But they in turn have caste rules and so on.

Political Limits: Some religious communities may wish to run their own governments within a territory, but this may not be possible because the political system can only function in a unified way. Religions which insist on setting up their separate governments test Hindu tolerance. Thus Zoroastrians, who did not go for that kind of thing at all, are more tolerated than the Christians who went for it in a limited way under the Portuguese and in a somewhat secular way under the British. And the Christians are more tolerated than the Muslims who sought political separation in a big way. Interestingly, until they made a bid for political power, the Muslims were tolerated with the same ease as the Zoroastrians and the Jews.

Rational Limits: Among some Hindu sects even the expectorations of a Guru were considered sacred which the followers tried to intercept. This is clearly unhygienic. Another sect, called Nikalsenis, used to venerate their British general, Nicholson and its members had themselves masochistically lashed. These instances seem symptomatic of religious pathology and are cases of religious enthusiasm overstepping the bounds of rational tolerance.

In my opinion Hinduism has created difficulties for itself from *within* by neglecting to observe the moral and rational limits of tolerance and from *without* by not taking into account the political limits of tolerance.

To conclude, *tolerance of tolerance* naturally appeals to Hinduism, but it has also unwisely displayed *tolerance of intolerance* by projecting its own internal ethos on other religions. Some of these have turned out to be *intolerant of tolerance* and have taken advantage of Hindu tolerance to undermine it. Hence I propose that, in the contemporary Indian setting, Hindus must develop *intolerance of intolerance*, and promote tolerance outside its own religious frontier by identifying and emphasizing the elements of tolerance in other religions. My study of comparative religion suggests that two strands can be identified in almost all the major religions of the world: a conservative one and a liberal one. This is true even of Hinduism. The difference lies in the relative strength of these forces, not in their absence or presence. Hinduism for our times therefore must aim at initiating an alliance among the liberal elements of all the religions of the world and in this way express its intolerance of intolerance and enhance tolerance of tolerance in a religiously pluralistic world. This is how Hindu pluralism can make a positive contribution in the context of a religiously pluralistic world. In other words, tolerance must be converted from a passive concept into an active one.

IV

One way of viewing the situation is in terms of the contrast between democracy and authoritarian regimes. Democracy is Hinduism in a political idiom. Totalitarian or authoritarian regimes are the political counterparts to the proselytizing religions like Islam and Christianity. Now, in the event of an actual conflict between democracies and totalitarian regimes, sometimes even democratic rights have to be suspended to fight totalitarian forces such as Nazism. Normally, when the crisis is over, these rights are restored. But consider a situation of prolonged conflict between the two, involving an indefinite suspension of democratic rights. The end result could well be that democracy gets trampled in the name of saving democracy. Thus, in order to save democracy, the totalitarian regimes must be kept under pressure to democratize, as seems to be the case in the current state of relationship between the USA and the USSR. In other words, in order to save *itself*, Hinduism must save others; that is, missionize other religions in the direction of tolerance. In general, no tolerant system can accept intolerance beyond the point when such intolerance will destroy that system itself which makes tolerance possible. Hinduism must guard against such self-destruction under the influence of misguided idealism.

Like a river, living Hinduism has changed its course during its passage through history many a time, though all the while moving forward steadily, even when running so deep as to appear still, towards the ocean of cosmic salvation. If one looks at the territory covered by Hinduism in history, one still finds signs of the old course it flowed by and if one digs deep enough one might still find water therein. Even when a river on a map seems to be flowing backwards towards its source (as might be said of some of the revivalistic movements within Hinduism) and sometimes even when the river seems to be moving away from the ocean in the opposite direction (as might be argued was the case with some developments within Hinduism such as Tantra), one can rest assured that it is still flowing towards the ocean. So has it been with Hinduism and, therefore, within it a poet can assert:

> As the different streams having their sources in different places all mingle their water in the sea, so, O Lord, the different paths which men take through different tendencies, various though they appear, crooked or straight, all lead to Thee.[2]

V

This verse was cited by Swami Vivekananda during his appearance at the World Parliament of Religions in 1893. The time has now come to ask: whither Hindu tolerance, hundred years after Vivekananda? To answer this question one must begin with Vivekananda.

Swami Vivekananda (1863–1902) is widely acknowledged

for identifying religious tolerance virtually as a defining characteristic of Hinduism.[3] He himself acknowledged his debt in this respect to the teachings of his guru Rāmakṛṣṇa (1836–1886). It has been observed, however, that his own teachings on this point diverge from those of Rāmakṛṣṇa in some respects. It is said, for instance, that he Advaitized Rāmakṛṣṇa's position on religious tolerance.[4] At this point I would like to indicate another direction in which he may have modified the teachings of Rāmakṛṣṇa, a modification which is of particular significance for contemporary developments in Hinduism, a hundred years after Vivekananda made his debut at the World Parliament of Religions in 1893.

An incident which occurred during his first visit to the USA sets the stage for introducing my argument. It occurred in the latter part of 1894 during his visit to Boston.

> It so happened that he once spoke in Boston before a large audience gathered to hear him on 'My Master'. Full of the fire of renunciation that he was, when he saw before him the audience composed, for the most part, of worldly-minded men and women lacking in spiritual sympathy and earnestness, he felt that it would be a desecration to speak to them of his understanding of, and his real feelings of devotion for Shri Ramakrishna. So, instead, he launched out on a terrible denunciation of the vulgar, physical and materialistic ideas which underlay the whole of Western civilisation. Hundreds of people left the hall abruptly, but in no way affected, he went on to the end. The next morning the papers were filled with varying criticisms, some highly favourable, others severely critical in their analysis of what he had said, but all commenting on his fearlessness, sincerity and frankness. When he himself read the report of his speech, he was stung with remorse. He wept bitterly for thus denouncing others and said, 'My Master could not see the evil side of a man. He had nothing but love even for his worst villifiers. It is nothing short of sacrilege on my part to abuse others and wound their feelings while speaking about my Master. Really I have not understood Shri Ramakrishna and am totally unfit to speak about him!'[5]

Why was Vivekananda so filled with remorse? He specifies the reason himself: He had wounded the feelings of others, something his Master abhorred. We must, however, delve deeper. Swami Vivekananda had lashed out earlier against Western materialism at the Parliament of Religions itself and without a trace of remorse. On 19 September 1893 while he was still at Chicago, 'in the morning sessions the Christian delegates, alarmed at the hearing that the oriental religions were receiving in every meeting, made a concerted attack on Hinduism'.[6] This attack provoked the following response from Swami Vivekananda:

> We who have come from the east have sat here day after day and have been told in a patronizing way that we ought to accept Christianity because Christian nations are the most prosperous. We look about us and we see England the most prosperous Christian nation in the world, with her foot upon the neck of 250,000,000 Asiatics. We look back into history and see that the prosperity of Christian Europe began with Spain. Spain's prosperity began with the invasion of Mexico. Christianity wins its prosperity by cutting the throats of its fellow men. At such a price the Hindoo will not have prosperity.[7]

Hence, what Swami Vivekananda was really remorseful about was not the fact that he had criticized Western civilization, but the fact that he had done so without provocation. This enables one to make a more general observation that for Rāmakṛṣṇa religious tolerance represented the absence of coercion, conversion and criticism in the relationship among religions; for Vivekananda it involved the absence of coercion and conversion but not of criticism, especially when such criticism was offered in response to an attack on one's tradition.

This point emerges clearly in the course of his dispute with the Brooklyn Centre of the Ramabai Circle with whom he joined issue on the question of the condition of widows, and of women in general in India. He described the women Christian propagandists who, according to him, indulged in wilful distortion and exaggeration in their portrayal of Hindu women, as 'churchies', 'awful fanatics' and 'titanesses'[8] (his words).

It seems a group of Christian missionaries, whose 'funds had decreased in one year by as much as one million pounds' as a result of 'Vivekananda's success', circulated a story that 'because of Vivekananda, Mrs. Bagley (the wife of the ex-Governor of Michigan) has had to dismiss a servant-girl; he is dreadfully intemperate'. Swami Vivekananda wrote in a letter on 21 March 1895:

I am astonished to hear the scandals the Ramabai Circle are indulging in about me. Among others, one item is that Mrs. Bagley of Detriot had to dismiss a servant-girl on account of my bad character!!! Don't you see, Mrs. Bull, that however a man may conduct himself, there will always be persons who will invent the blackest lies about him. At Chicago I had such things spread every day against me.

And these women are invariably the very Christian of Christians!...[9]

It seems that on another occasion:

certain parties, securing the photograph of his Master, managed to have it printed in one of the leading papers of a large Mid-Western city, together with slurring comments upon his appearance and upon Hinduism and Hindu Yogis in general. Then he was heard to exclaim, 'Oh! This *is* BLASPHEMY!'[10]

Even when not directly provoked, Swami Vivekananda did not hesitate to criticize Christianity. The following extract from a newspaper report is instructive:

When someone suggested to him that Christianity was a saving power, he opened his great dark eyes upon him and said, 'If Christianity is a saving power in itself, why has it not saved the Ethiopians, the Abyssinians?' He also arraigned our own crimes, the horror of women on the stage, the frightful immorality in our streets, our drunkenness, our thieving, our political degeneracy, the murdering in our West, the lynching in our South, and we, remembering his own Thugs, were still too delicate to mention them.[11]

A much more dramatic incident occurred on his voyage home after his first visit to the West.

There were on the boat, among other passengers, two Christian missionaries who, in the course of a heated discussion with the Swami, lost their tempers and savagely criticized the Hindu religion. The Swami walked to one of them, seized him by the collar, and said menacingly, 'If you abuse my religion again, I will throw you overboard.'

'Let me go, sir,' the frightened missionary apologized; 'I'll never do it again.'

Later, in the course of a conversation with a disciple in Calcutta, he asked, 'What would you do if someone insulted your mother?' The disciple answered, 'I would fall upon him, sir, and teach him a good lesson.'

'Bravo!' said the Swami. 'Now, if you had the same positive feeling for your religion, your true mother, you could never see any Hindu brother converted to Christianity. Yet you see this occurring every day, and you are quite indifferent. Where is your faith? Where is your patriotism? Every day Christian missionaries abuse Hinduism to your face, and yet how many are there amongst you whose blood boils with righteous indignation and who will stand up in its defense?'[12]

It is clear that for Swami Vivekananda Hindu tolerance did not include tolerance of hostile criticism of Hinduism. In fact, one can go even a step further and say that Hindu religious tolerance as visualized by Swami Vivekananda included intolerance of intolerance. The *London Daily Chronicle* records that in his public lecture at Prince's Hall in London on 22 October 1895, Swami Vivekananda 'denounced our commercial prosperity, our bloody wars and our religious intolerance ...'[13]

To conclude, it might be well to focus more closely on the dialectic between tolerance and intolerance. Four logical combinations naturally suggest themselves: (1) Tolerance of tolerance; (2) Intolerance of intolerance; (3) Tolerance of intolerance; and (4) Intolerance of tolerance.

For Rāmakṛṣṇa Hindu religious tolerance included options (1) and (3) and excluded options (2) and (4). For Swami Vivekananda religious tolerance included options (1) and (2) and excluded option (3), which he did not avail of himself, and option (4), often adopted by Christian critics of Hinduism. By opening up the Hindu self-definition of tolerance to include the 'double negation' of the third option 'intolerance of intolerance', Swami Vivekananda imparted to Hindu tolerance a combative edge.

VI

However, one must ask the question: what actual form does this intolerance of intolerance assume in Hinduism? The form it assumes most acutely is Hinduism's antipathy to religious conversion or what it regards as the illogic of conversion.

The doctrine of conversion implies the acceptance of one thing and the rejection of another. In a sense this phenomenon is a fact of life: The acceptance of the good involves the rejection of the bad; the acceptance of virtue involves the rejection of vice. This is true in an even profounder sense. It has been said, for instance, that 'the condition of existence is struggle; the conflict not only of good and bad but of relative good with relative good'. However, in another sense the statement that acceptance must involve rejection is not true, for the acceptance of virtue, while it requires the rejection of vice, does not entail the rejection of another virtue.

The so-called missionary religions of the world understand the acceptance of conversion only in the first sense and are therefore compelled to regard religions other than their own as bad or vicious, or at least relatively so. But what is needed is not conversion from one religion to another but reconversion to one's own religion, for although we are in them they are not in us, or conversely, they are in us and we are not in them. It must always be someone who speaks for all; this predicament of universal religion is transformed into a claim by a missionary religion. In a sense, of course, every religious tradition is missionary. It is an expression of itself and by that very fact serves as an example to others, a collective realization of Hillel's famous self-realization: 'If I am not for myself who will be for me; and if I am only for myself then who am I?' Therefore, by merely being itself rather than for itself an authentic religious tradition proclaims its mission. In order, therefore, to be authentically missionary a religion does not have to be missionary, it just has to be. There is a difference between being good and doing good. Being good will naturally manifest itself in doing good, for 'one does what one is; one becomes what one does' and as one does what one is the cycle of virtue is sufficient unto itself. But if we do good with a motive and if that motive is to convert someone to one's faith, then it amounts to giving a bad name to doing good. Therefore, if to *be* is to be missionary in the best sense of the term, then to try to be missionary is not to be so at all; it is to make what should be natural artificial, and in trying to make the artificial appear as natural one only succeeds in making it more so.

VII

However, we must now take into account a crucial consideration that the structural as opposed to the philosophical basis of

Hindu attitude to conversion is isomorphic with its attitude towards caste.

Ever since Hinduism became known in the West in modern times, two of its aspects have claimed a good deal of attention: (1) the caste system[14] and (2) Hindu reluctance to convert people of other religions on the ground that all religions are valid.[15] The former has, in general, been vigorously condemned[16] and the latter enthusiastically applauded.[17] *It seems to have gone unnoticed that these two aspects of Hinduism are logically connected.*

Although a wide range of attitudes exists in Hinduism towards the caste system, the dominant view alone need be outlined here. According to this view, Hindu society was divided into four varṇas. These were the Brāhmaṇa, the Kṣatriya, the Vaisya and the Śudra. There was none who was outside the pale of this scheme.[18]

The nature of the relationship between the varṇas was hierarchical, in accordance with the order outlined above. All the varṇas had a given set of duties and responsibilities.[19] Marriage was to take place within one's varṇa.[20] Thus, the key aspect of the scheme is that (1) caste was based on birth and (2) lasted till death. One was born into a particular varṇa in accordance with the karma of previous life or lives, and although one could change one's varṇa over the course of several lives, indeed in the very next life, the varṇa in the course of a particular existence had to be regarded as, by and large, immutable. Again, the change of varṇa the next time took place at *birth* and remained unaltered throughout the rest of that life. This further highlights the role of birth in the determination of varṇa. It is helpful to recognize here that the varṇa scheme is, in essence, a classificatory schema. It classifies four types and by being born into one type one came to belong to a certain varṇa.

This then is the classical picture of the varṇa scheme as visualized, and perhaps idealized, by the standard *Dharmaśāstras*.[21]

Now, the Hindu attitude to conversion may be examined. Why is it that Hinduism discourages conversion from one religion to another—including conversion not only *from* but *to* Hinduism? These reasons were clearly articulated by Śrī Chandraśekhara Bhāratī Swāmī during the course of an interview with an American who was keen to convert to Hinduism but was being dissuaded by the Swāmī. The Swāmī told him:

> It is no freak that you were born a Christian. God ordained it that way because by the *samskara* acquired through your actions (*karma*) in previous births your soul has taken a pattern which will find its richest fulfilment in the Christian way of life. Therefore your salvation lies there and not in some other religion. What you must change is not your faith but your life.[22]

If these remarks are analysed it will be found that in this view the fact that one belongs to a particular religion was based on birth, in accordance with one's past karma and would last till death.[23] If now it is recognized that the various religions are in essence a classificatory schema for typing people according to their beliefs and practices, then the close parallel between the Hindu attitude towards caste and the Hindu attitude towards conversion becomes apparent. Both involve a classificatory commitment on the basis of birth.

This is not to say that there are no differences involved. The classical varṇa classification is hierarchical, whereas the classification involving the major religions has no *fixed* hierarchy—each religion can place itself at the top of the heap. Caste is largely a matter of orthopraxy, faith a matter more of orthodoxy. Other differences could also be identified. But the similarity in the ideological orientation nevertheless remains striking. The same birth-ascription which accounts for the Hindu attitude towards caste, underwrites the Hindu attitude towards conversion. There seems to be a strong logical connection between the two based on the doctrine of karma and rebirth when applied within a classificatory framework.[24]

VIII

This connection between caste and tolerance is so significant that it calls for further investigation. The usual form it has assumed sees the rigidity of the caste system as a trade-off for

Hinduism's doctrinal openness. In other words, Hinduism's polydoxy is at least connected with and sometimes even traced to its orthopraxy in terms of caste. For instance, Klaus K. Klostermaier observes that 'Hinduism may appear to be very vague and extremely tolerant to the outsider, but the insider must conform to very precise regulations of life within the group', whether they be of caste or sect.[25] While there may be some truth in this to which others have drawn attention as well, it should not obscure the larger reality that Hinduism is characterized by a plurality of *both* doctrines and practices to such a degree that the insight possesses limited application.

We must move to another level to examine the broader implications of this relationship, in the spirit that the broader explanation must account for the limited insight even as it opens up fresh paradigmatic horizons. Such a result might be achieved by subjecting the relationship to a systemic analysis—such as that between the whole and the parts. The enabling insight here seems to be that the whole can be equal to, more than, or less than the sum of the parts. This calls for elaboration.

The case of the whole being equal to the sum of the parts is exemplified by any authentic case of dual citizenship, as it were. In a federal democracy, for instance, a citizen is simultaneously a citizen of a state and of the union of these states— and is equally so. A comparable example from a religious system would perhaps be provided by one's membership of a religious tradition and of a sect within it at the same time. In a Hiṅdu version of the Christian view that Jesus was fully man and fully God one could claim that one is both an Advaitin (or a Viśiṣṭādvaitin or a Dvaitin) and a Hindu at the same time or a Hindu as well as a Vaiṣṇava, a Śaiva or a Śākta at the same time. The relationship between the parts and the whole within Hinduism, when it comes to tolerance and to caste, is not of this type. I venture to suggest that in the case of tolerance the whole is greater than the sum of the parts—that Hindu tolerance spills over beyond Hinduism as it were. An illustration might help clarify this point.

A verse found in collections of 'well-turned sayings' or

subhāṣitas[26] and identified by S. Radhakrishnan as written by the tenth-century Hindu thinker, Udayana,[27] is often cited as textual evidence of Hindu tolerance. It translates:

May Hari, the Lord of the three worlds, bestow on you the desired reward, whom the Śaivas worship as Śiva, Vedāntins as *Brahman*, the Bauddhas as Buddha, the Naiyāyikas proficient in the means of knowledge as the Creator, those devoted to Jain teachings as Arhat and Mīmāṁsakas as Yajña.[28]

The verse is significant in that it straddles over the sectarian distinctions such as between Śaiva and Vaiśṇava and the philosophical distinctions between the *āstika* (orthodox) and *nāstika* (non-orthodox) schools of Indian thought. However, the story does not stop here. After offering his own translation of the text, S. Radhakrishnan adds: *'If he had been writing in this age, he would have added "whom the Christians devoted to work as Christ and the Mohammedans as Allah".'*[29] Raḍhakrishnan even undertakes to enlarge the quatrain by adding a fifth line in Sanskrit: *kraistvāḥ krīstur iti kriyāpararatāḥ alleti māhammadāḥ.*[30]

Clearly then, Hindu tolerance has overflowed the accepted boundaries of Hinduism, just as a river might overflow its banks. It is in this sense that when it comes to tolerance, or better still, acceptance of other religions, Hinduism tends to be more than the sum of its parts. Some would even say, recalling the idiom of the *Gītā*, that it might consider itself merely a part in a whole, a mere tank when there is water everywhere.

The caste system in Hinduism represents a case in which the whole is *less* than the sum of the parts, in the sense that while there is perfect equality within a caste it does not extend to the relationship among castes. Hindu tolerance must then address this asymmetry, if we are to make full sense of Hinduism as a religious system. Hindu tolerance is incomplete without full acceptance of the people themselves and cannot stop short at the full acceptance of their beliefs and practices. The real issue is not that caste serves as a centripetal pragmatic centre to the centrifugal, doctrinally expanding if not exploding circumference of the Hindu universe, the central issue is why the social concentric circle has lagged behind and not caught up with the ideological. In a nutshell, if Hinduism could develop the concept of choosing one's own deity or that of *iṣṭadevatā* then what prevented it from evolving the doctrine of *iṣṭavarṇatā* or the choosing of one's own occupation?

The question is a stupendous one but one can venture a historical answer. It is well known that Hindu thought underwent a major shift when the majority opinion in the tradition veered round to the view that, in terms of thought, primacy was to be accorded to the later and not the earlier portions of the Vedas—to the Vedānta and not the Mīmāṁsā, or alternatively to *uttaramīmāṁsā* and not *pūrvamīmāṁsā*. However, although this shift did occur in the realm of thought, it was not followed through by a similar shift in the realm of social practice. A well-known line, often recited in *paṇḍita* circles, avers that 'the former part of the Vedas is explained by the Dharmaśāstras and the epics and Purāṇas expatiate on the latter'.[31] But if the organization of thought has shifted to the latter portions—the Upaniṣads—where are the Dharmaśāstras which correspond to an accompanying shift in social organization? In other words, Hindu society has lagged behind Hindu philosophy, just as Śaṅkara's conduct towards the outcaste lagged behind his own Advaitic beliefs—a fact which the outcaste reminded him of when he asked him to move away.[32]

But how is this transition to be effected. As is often the case, if Hinduism is part of the problem, it is often also part of the solution. The *locus classicus* of the varṇa system is the Puruṣa-sūkta, although the word varṇa does not appear therein. In and of itself, as many including Mahatma Gandhi pointed out, the hymn does not enjoin subordination but rather coordination, and perhaps represents a stage when Hindu philosophical and social realities were not as divorced as they were destined to become.

By the time of classical Hinduism as embodied in the Manusmṛti, however, the situation had changed. But if one looks closely at the Manusmṛti it also implies that the situation can be changed again—and in an egalitarian way. It may sound incredible to begin with, that 'the much-maligned Manu' may have something therapeutic rather than pathological to offer. I shall therefore present the evidence and let the reader be the judge.

When Manu introduces the discussion of the caste system he refers to the Puruṣasūkta, stating clearly that the four varṇas emerged, in that order, from the limbs of the cosmic being. But he prefaces this with a gloss entirely absent in the *Ṛg Vedic* text he cites, namely, that this happened in this way for the sake of the prosperity of the people or *lokānāṁ tu vivridhyartham* (I.31) to cite the text. We are thus provided a criterion by which to assess the phenomenon. If this statement is read with another in Manu that even Vedic dharma may be abandoned if it has gone to seed as it were and become the subject of denunciation by the people (*lokavikruṣṭa*), as is clearly stated in verse 176 of chapter IV, then it is clear this is what should be done even to the caste system if it has earned that odium.

This enables us to see the relationship between caste and tolerance in a new light. Caste is not the shadow side of Hindu tolerance nor is it merely the regrettably less radiant dimension of an otherwise tolerant tradition—it is that dimension of the tradition which had not yet been exposed to the thorough X-ray of its radiation rather than radiance. When this is done the karmic nexus between caste and tolerance becomes clear and one is led beyond the relationships usually postulated. Two such relationships were explored in this section. According to one view, Hindu doctrinal tolerance was correlated to Hindu caste intolerance in a sort of a symbiotic relationship. The suggestion is attractive but its initial formulation must be followed by an eventual historical reservation, that in the more dynamic periods of Hinduism doctrinal flexibility and caste mobility have often gone hand in hand.[33] According to the second view, Hinduism was involved not in a trade-off between spiritual openness and social inegalitarianism but was involved in a systemically non-reciprocal relationship in their own distinctive spheres. Both of these views—that of mutual correlation or appositional coexistence—seem to lack the integral cohesiveness of the original insight that both doctrinal inclusiveness and caste-exclusiveness were radically interconnected through a birth-ascriptive interpretation of the doctrine of karma and we will therefore hold on to that explanation.

IX

In order to continue to hold on to it, however, we must now also test it from a comparative perspective. According to this perspective the correlation between doctrinal flexibility and caste inflexibility proposed as an explanation of their apparently simultaneous presence in the case of Hinduism, is a specific illustration of a more general phenomenon which characterizes the relationship between religion and ideology, and society or social organization in general; these tend to be oppositional either within a society itself or across different societies. Thus, the same opposition between doctrinal openness and social rigidity found within a society may also be found transpositionally in a culture which is both doctrinally and socially egalitarian within itself but uncharitable towards cultures outside its orbit. The patronage of Latin American dictatorships by a democratic America would illustrate this point.

This trend of thought has led some to postulate that there lies 'the *deepest* dialectics' at the heart of the matter, 'a dialectics of human ideals of *good society* and *good religion*: the more classless, equality-hungry it is, the more imperialistic and intolerant of the *other* society it becomes'.[34]

To place this discussion in a proper perspective we need to recall that we examined three possible relationships between tolerance and caste: (1) as karmically co-originative; (2) as oppositionally correlational and (3) as systematically disjunctive. One must now put alongside these three views the fourth possibility of dialectical opposition. Unless this is satisfactorily accounted for our preferred karmic explanation would remain under a cloud.

One notices a similarity between this position and the proposal of oppositional correlation between social inflexibility and doctrinal flexibility within Hinduism: the two go hand in hand. What is more, it can be historically supported by the examples of both capitalism and communism. Thus, one could argue that while on the one hand the 'free society' of the USA is held together by an *absolutized* American way of life within it, or alternatively by its preference for dealing with *absolutist* governments outside it, on the other hand the classless communist societies were precisely the ones which were intolerant of other societies which they sought to bring under the sway of the communist empire, or alternatively that their social egalitarianism went hand in hand with political authoritarianism. K.N. Iengar, who accepts the view that 'the rigidity of the Hindu social order is compensated for by the flexibility of its modes of worship' goes on to suggest that we should 'contrast this with the egalitarian societies of Fascists and Communists which required compulsory worship and obedience of their dictator on pain of death for questioning the authority of his politburo, composed of casteless bipeds'.[35]

The key to the paradox is provided by the word dialectics. While one meaning of the word dialectic restricts its semantic scope to '*opposing* forces', the more philosophical sense of the word indicates the following sense: that if you probe phenomena deep enough you will find that the phenomena owe their existence to a *contradiction.* If this distinction between dialectics as opposition and dialectics as contradiction is kept in mind, it opens the door to another possibility. A good religion, which believes in equality, and realizes it within its own society, will not then owe its existence to the opposition of an inegalitarian society or/and religion it might face. It will, however, perceive its contradiction within it which it will try to remove by introducing the same egalitarianism in the other society by its own example. This hunger for equality is a unique kind of hunger—it devours itself like the mythical *kīrtimukha* of Hindu mythology![36] We may also remind ourselves at this point of the wisdom of Buddha's view that while we may hold certain views we may not cling to them, specially when evidence—in this case contemporary—begins to render them more and more questionable.

Chapter 5

Hinduism and the Future

I

In the preceding chapters we set out to place Hinduism in the context of our times. In doing so we discovered that there is a dialectical relationship between the religious traditions and the times: the traditions sometimes mould or seek to mould the times and are sometimes moulded by the times. We identified the caste system as an item in regard to which most Hindu leaders thought, with the remarkable exception of Gandhi, that Hinduism should allow itself to be moulded by the times. Mahatma Gandhi wanted to mould the world in accordance with his vision of the varṇa system. Our conclusion was that once a *dynamic* understanding of karma is accepted neither the traditional vision nor the Gandhian vision of varṇa could be sustained, and that Hinduism had to change with the times.

While in one respect Hinduism was to be changed by the times, in another respect it was to change the times—with respect to promoting religious tolerance. We discovered, however, that the traditional basis of caste and of tolerance were identical—they were both based on birth. The dissolution of caste also meant, if not the dissolution of Hindu tolerance then, certainly, the dissolution of its traditional basis. One needs to dwell on this point even at the risk of some repetition. The convergence in the Hindu attitude towards caste and conversion possesses far-reaching implications which are not immediately obvious but which are potentially revolutionary and need to be spelled out clearly. The Hindu attachment to caste and its antipathy to conversion are both based on the acceptance of birth-ascription. They are two sides of the same coin. And birth-ascription, as noted earlier, implies a *static* concept of karma. Such a static concept of karma, we argued, is now no longer viable as Hinduism changes with the times and adopts a *dynamic* concept of karma. The dissolution of the traditional caste system will then also be accompanied by the dissolution of the traditional basis of Hindu tolerance. Hinduism will ultimately become a casteless and missionary religion instead of remaining a caste-bound and tolerant entity. To get rid of caste is also to get rid of tolerance. This is then the great dilemma. Caste should go. If caste goes, Hindu tolerance goes with it as the basis of both is the same. It is inevitable that, with a dynamic concept of karma in place, Hinduism will also become a missionary religion like Christianity and Islam.

If such is the case does Hinduism have anything to offer to the world, even of providing it a new direction, much less changing it? In my view Hinduism still has a role to play in changing the times and this role is still the traditional one of promoting religious harmony. But it has to be provided with a new basis to replace the traditional one. The nature of its difference from Christianity and Islam will no longer consist of the fact that they are missionary religions which Hinduism is not, but rather in the fact that while Hinduism is also a missionary religion, its sense of mission sets it apart from them.

The saving insight, it seems to me, consists in this: that while the transformation of Hinduism from an ethnic to a missionary religion cannot be prevented if caste dissolves, its *sense of mission* may still be defined in such a way as differs from that of other religions, so that it remains universalistic instead of becoming particularistic, promotes tolerance and brings about peace among the religions of the world. This calls for a thorough revisioning of our attitude to religion itself. I shall elaborate upon these remarks at two levels: A philosophical one and a pedagogical one. This bifurcation of levels does not involve a duality in terms of the goal which remains the attainment of religious peace. Hans Küng has remarked that there will be no peace among nations so long as there is no peace among religions. And let me also add to this the wry comment of Helen Keller: I do not want the peace that passeth understanding: I want that understanding which brings peace.

The Philosophical Dimension

The conceptual spaces that Hinduism provides for tolerance seem to be endless. The question of tolerance only arises in the context of the other, so let us start in the state of pristine purity in which there exists only one entity identical with itself. In such a situation the question of tolerance does not arise at all. There is no *other*, either to be tolerated or not to be tolerated. Let us now initiate the process of differentiation from this state of original unity. The process of differentiation means that a distinct entity apart from the original comes into being. However, distinction need not necessarily imply difference. I am not saying that the second object is a clone of the first; it is distinct from the first in both space as well as in form. However, distinction need not imply separation. The various parts of a tree are distinct but not separate. Or, in other words, distinction need not imply division. Radhakrishnan had said that we may divide in order to distinguish but we may not distinguish in order to divide. We divide the various parts of a country into distinct regions on a map but we do not draw these distinctions to cause divisions among them. Thus, even if distinction leads to differentiation, it need not lead to disagreement. The fact that the human species is differentiated between male and female does not mean that the two, *ipso facto*, must disagree.

Let us suppose, however, that distinction has led to disagreement; in that case it does not automatically follow that disagreement must lead to discord. Many have been known to agree to disagree. However, let us suppose that the downward slide continues, and that disagreement does lead to discord. If such be the case then discord need not necessarily lead to confrontation. There is still room for discordant concord. In an orchestra, not everyone may be playing the right tune but people don't come to blows over it. However, if the situation is permitted to deteriorate even further, even then it need not end up in a conflictual situation—there is still a stop of peace on the way. The situation may end in one of concordant discord. In terms of the metaphor of the orchestra, concord has now broken down into discord but the concordant notes can still predominate. There could be heated debate among colleagues which, however, stops short of rupturing concord. Sects within a religion could easily coexist in states of discordant concord or concordant discord.

Let the situation deteriorate even further. Let us assume that the breakdown has led to confrontation. Confrontation, however, need not necessarily lead to conflict. Even when troops have been known to confront each other conflict has been prevented from breaking out. However, let the breakdown continue. Let us suppose that conflict has broken out. However, conflict need not inevitably lead to violence. Apart from the 'passive aggression' psychologists talk about or the 'aggressive pacifism' of a Gandhi who would undertake a fast to death, parties to a conflict have often been known to resort to courts. There are numerous techniques of judicial conflict resolution such as arbitration, collective bargaining, etc.

Let us travel further down the lane of the worst-case scenario. Let us suppose that conflict has led to violence. However, violence may not lead to combat. The party being subjected to violence may refuse to retaliate! Let us suppose, however, that retaliation does occur. In that case, combat need not necessarily lead to war. It is known, for instance, that certain tribes choose to resolve disputes by single combat to spare the bloodshed of a general war. However, let us suppose that general combat has taken place, leading to war. Even once war has commenced, however, it need not be carried to the bitter end; it may end in a truce.

The point is that it is misleading to think of war and peace in terms of black and white. There is a lot of grey area to grope in, as it were, wherein one could come to terms. The dualistic mode of thinking in terms of the excluded middle tends to exclude the whole middle zone of possible peace.

Thinking in terms of a continuum rather than clear-cut binary options is characteristic of Hinduism and conducive to peace. It is a characteristic of the attitude of tolerance to move along this continuum and make a happy stop somewhere on the way before one falls off the cliff or runs into a cul-de-sac. To sum up, distinction need not lead to division, division need not lead to disagreement, disagreement need not lead to discord, discord need not lead to conflict, conflict need not lead to violence, violence need not lead to war, war need not lead to annihilation of the other for the original monadic peace to be restored.

II

The Pedagogical Dimension

I would like to begin this section with a comment with which Louis Renou, the French Indologist, ends one of his short surveys of Hinduism. He wrote in 1962:

> Hinduism, however—except perhaps in certain Tântric systems—is not esoteric. By the very fact that there is possibility of choice among diverse paths and various techniques, Truth is for Hinduism an indivisible treasure; spiritual immediacy is widely distributed, the mystic path is open to everyone. In its purest forms, this religion becomes a type of wisdom, that wisdom which impressed the ancient Greeks when they visited India and which could be of some fruitfulness again for our blasé cultures. It is as wisdom that we should like to define Hinduism rather than by the equivocal term *spirituality.*
>
> One is never bound to predict the future; and today the future of a nation is no longer in its hands alone. Still it is likely that the Indian caste system will disappear sooner or later and with it will disappear certain crude Indian institutions. There will survive then a way of thought freed of social contingencies, one which will be endowed with unforeseen powers of maturity.[1]

I would specially like to draw attention to what is said at the beginning and at the end of the passage. Hinduism, it is said, is not esoteric but *caste was.* If this is kept in mind then the unforeseen powers of maturity with which Hinduism might become endowed in the post-caste age are not as unforeseeable as Renou makes them out to be. It now becomes possible to assert that the transformation of Hinduism will infuse it with a *spiritual* missionary vitality, notwithstanding the fact that Renou prefers the word wisdom to spirituality.

This *spiritual* orientation of Hinduism essentially consists in its openness in the matter of spiritual pursuit—which incidentally Renou is quick to recognize himself. This should be contrasted with the more *ideological* orientation of other religions which impels them to convert others. The crucial move, as Hinduism becomes missionary, would then consist of making it a vehicle of diffusing a spiritual as opposed to an ideological orientation of religion around the world. Since spirituality knows no religious barriers, it would then be the destiny of Hinduism to spread its message of universalism around the world.

What is to be the content of such universalism? Let us begin by stating what it is *not* going to be, what it does *not* mean. It does *not* mean the conversion of the world to Hinduism. It does *not* mean the establishment of a universal religion which replaces all other religions. We know that religious barriers exist. It means the conversion of these barriers into bridges. This is to be achieved by promoting the realization that *all* the religions of the world are the heritage of *each* human being. This goal can be achieved by *promoting the study of all religions as one's own, so that we stop regarding our own religion as the only true one.* Mahatma Gandhi wrote in 1926:

I hold that it is the duty of every cultured man or woman to read sympathetically the scriptures of the world. If we are to respect others' religions as we would have them to respect our own, a friendly study of the world's religions is a sacred duty. We need not dread, upon our grown up children, the influence of scriptures other than our own. We liberalize their outlook upon life by encouraging them to study freely all that is clean. Fear there would be when some one reads his own scriptures to young people with the intention secretly or openly of converting them. He must then be biased in favour of his own scriptures. For myself, I regard my study of and reverence for the Bible, the Quran, and the other scriptures to be wholly consistent with my claim to be a staunch *Sanatani* Hindu. He is no *Sanatani* Hindu who is narrow, bigoted, and considers evil to be good if it has the sanction of antiquity and is to be found supported in any Sanskrit book. I claim to be a staunch *Sanatani* Hindu because, though I reject all that offends my moral sense, I find the Hindu scriptures to satisfy the needs of the soul. My respectful study of our religions has not abated my reverence for or my faith in the Hindu scriptures. They have indeed left their deep mark upon my understanding of the Hindu scriptures. They have broadened my view of life. They have enabled me to understand more clearly many an obscure passage in the Hindu scriptures.[2]

When one wants to spread a message in the world it must be spread *from* somewhere, and that somewhere must be India. The study of all the religions of the world must be made compulsory throughout India. It is often said that the mantle of Mahatma Gandhi fell on the shoulders of Pandit Nehru. In the present context, however, it fell on the shoulders of Maulana Abul Kalam Azad. In January 1948 Maulana Azad declared:

If we want to safeguard the intellectual life of our country against this danger [of fanaticism], it becomes all the more necessary for us not to leave the imparting of early religious education to private sources. We should rather take it under our direct care and supervision. No doubt, a foreign government had to keep itself away from religious education. But a national government cannot divest itself of undertaking this responsibility.[3]

Pandit Nehru, however, 'strongly disagreed with this proposal. The Constituent Assembly also disagreed, and so Article 28 (1) of the Constitution of 1950 simply states: "No religious instruction shall be provided in any educational institution wholly maintained out of state funds"'.[4]

The matter was revived by the University Education Commission of 1948–49, headed by Dr S. Radhakrishnan. It asserted that 'if we exclude spiritual training from our institutions we would be untrue to our whole historical development'. It recommended that:

(1) all educational institutions start work with a few minutes for silent meditation;

(2) in the first year of the Degree course lives of the great religious leaders like Gautama the Buddha, Confucius, Zoroaster, Socrates, Jesus, Śaṅkara, Rāmānuja, Madhva, Mohammad, Kabīr, Nānak, Gāndhi, be taught;

(3) in the second year some selections of a universalist character from the scriptures of the world be studied;
(4) in the third year, the central problems of the philosophy of religion be considered.[5]

The recommendations were never implemented.

Donald Eugene Smith reduces the reasoning involved in the above-mentioned suggestions to four basic propositions: '(1) dogmatic religion leads to conflict; (2) religious conflict leads to the secular state; (3) the secular state bans only dogmatic religious instruction in state schools; (4) the state can and should provide for the teaching of universal religion.'[6] He then goes on to say:

> The four recommendations made by the commission are in themselves unobjectionable. A few moments of silent meditation each day could not possibly harm anyone. No one would deny that a balanced university curriculum might very well include the study of the great men of religious history, the various religious books, and the philosophy of religion. *What is disturbing is the fact that these subjects are all to be taught from a particular point of view, determined by the doctrinal assumptions of neo-Hinduism.* This being the case, scholarly objectivity as well as religious neutrality are bound to suffer. The Koran, like the *Ṛg Veda*, will be made to teach that 'the Real is one; sages call it by various names,' for the commission has already announced that 'this is the teaching of Islam when taken in its profoundest sense.'[7]

He adverts to this fear again later.[8]

I would like to suggest that this fear is very Western in nature. The fear that the knowledge of various religions will destroy one's religion in the name of some universal religion or cause *dharmasaṅkara* as it were, is as baseless as the classical Hindu fear that the abolition of caste distinctions would destroy Hindu society, through *varṇa-saṅkara*, the fear Arjuna nervously voices at the beginning of the *Gītā*[9]

In my view this has always been Hinduism's mission: to bring what is outside of history and time within it; to temporalize the timeless, to pinpoint the omnipresent so that our attitude to what is present in time and space may change and become self-elevating and all-embracing. At this juncture in its history this goal is best achieved by it for itself and for all by getting rid of boundaries between religions, as barriers dividing them, while at the same time retaining them as field markers which facilitate our movements in the spiritual terrain. I feel that this has always been Hinduism's mission as it spread over this country and brought together all the existing elements of its religiosity in a close embrace; or shall we say, wove them into a fabric of such tremendous tensile strength that when the receding hands of a retreating destiny tried to grab it away they could rent it but could not remove it. Hinduism was distracted from its mission when self-doubts in the form of dissonant movements of thought assailed it from within in the form of Buddhism and Jainism. By the time it recovered its poise to resume its march it was thrown off its balance by virtually knock-out blows from without in its encounter with Islam and Christianity. Hinduism is now trying to shake off the dust and to stand on its feet at the moment. Once it is firmly on its feet it will realize that the Hinduism of our times calls for a change of pace and direction. While locked in a struggle for survival it misinterpreted this fact of history and internalized it as nature—as its ethnic nature. It must emerge from the chrysalis of this self-misunderstanding and once more resume its mission of spreading peace. What it has accomplished in the *temporal* dimension—by surviving the onslaughts of history, it must now surpass in the *spatial* dimension, by thriving in a religiously pluralistic world and by making it thrive.

The goal is glorious, but the means of attaining it seem to lack lustre—that of introducing the compulsory study of all the religions of the world, without fear or favour, in the national curricula. Could something so pedagogical achieve a mission so historical? It can. Just consider the unattractiveness of the seed compared to the flower; the crude nature of the electrical wirings which ultimately enable the room to be flooded with light; the ungainly pregnancy which precedes the arrival of a new life. Let us not make the fatal error of misjudging the fruits by the look of the roots.

Even the Constitution does not stand in the way of introducing such a respectful study of the religions of the world into our curricula; it is our misinterpretation of it and the talismanic misuse of the world secularism which stands in the way. In the theory of secularism we notice the distinction between two interpretations of it—along the lines of the 'wall of separation' and along the lines of the 'no-preference' clause. The no-preference clause is negatively phrased but it need not possess a negative connotation. In fact, it can and should be imparted a positive connotation. And even if the Constitution comes in the way then it should be changed. For 'new occasions teach new duties', as the poet says, and 'time makes ancient good uncouth' and sometimes even deadly. Let us not confer on the Constitution the immutability we denied even to the *sanātana dharma*.

The issues which Hinduism in our times faces are issues it has faced at all times. It cannot be otherwise, for if 'eternity is eternity it must be present here right now as well'.[10] Nor are these issues as such unique to Hinduism. Their contour may be specific to Hinduism but the landscape is shared by all religions of the world. Perhaps this too cannot be otherwise, for if the universal is truly universal it must be present in every particular being. But to descend from the higher heights of philosophy to the lower spaces, which support the higher places, the problem of religious peace which Hinduism faces in India is also faced by other religions of the world. But if religion is a part of the problem it can also be a part of the solution and if intolerance is infectious, tolerance too can be contagious. If war can break out, so can peace.

In my opinion, it is Hinduism's mission in our times to transform our religious understanding in such a way as to hasten the day when each individual will consider himself or herself the legatee of the entire religious heritage of humanity, warts and all; when he or she will move as freely among the religions of the world as he or she now moves, unfettered by self-consciousness, among the denominations of his or her own religion; when the difference between Ka'ba and Kāśī and Jerusalem will be merely geographical and when a Hindu will be proud to define himself or herself as one who is not; that even when one permits oneself to be defined, one refuses to be confined. While the proselytizing religions of the world aspire to be accepted by the whole of humanity, the aspiration of Hinduism, by contrast, is much more modest; instead of aspiring to be accepted by the whole of humanity, it merely aspires to accept the whole of humanity.

To conclude then: Hinduism must be shaped by those whose religion it is, by the masses and not by the classes. It should be a free association of independent and equal individuals. The horizon of its doctrine of karma and rebirth must be fused with the present to infuse it with contemporary relevance. The doctrine of varṇa should now apply to the individual instead of society and that of āśrama should span a day of life rather than a lifetime. Hinduism's *raison d'être* should continue to be tolerance which, like Einstenian space, should be unbounded but not infinite, and its mission in the world should remain what it has always been—the acceptance of all the religions of the world by all human beings as the inalienable religious heritage of every human being.

Notes

Chapter 1
Contemporary Hinduism: Its Sources and Resources

1. S. Radhakrishnan, *The Hindu View of Life* (New York: Macmillan Company, 1927), pp. 91–2.

2. Ibid., p. 42.

3. *The Complete Works of Swami Vivekananda* (Mayavati Memorial Edition, Calcutta: Advaita Ashrama, 1979), vol. III, p. 277.

4. M.K. Gandhi, *Hindu Dharma*, Bharatan Kumarappa, ed., (Ahmedabad: Navajivan Press, 1950), p. 231.

5. Ibid., p. 15.

6. Robert Ellsberg, *Gandhi on Christianity* (Maryknoll, New york: Orbis Books, 1991), p. 57.

7. T.M.P. Mahadevan, *Outlines of Hinduism* (Bombay: Chetana, 1971), p. 20.

8. Gandhi, *Hindu Dharma*, p. 237.

9. Ibid., p. 238. Elsewhere Mahatma Gandhi even extended the metaphor to Mother India (ibid., 232): 'There is in Hinduism room enough for Jesus, as there is for Mohammed, Zoroaster and Moses. For me the different religions are beautiful flowers from the same garden, or they are branches of the same majestic tree. Therefore they are equally true, though being received and interpreted through human instruments equally imperfect. It is impossible for me to reconcile myself to the idea of conversion after the style that goes on in India and elsewhere today. It is an error which is perhaps the greatest impediment to the world's progress towards peace. "Warring creeds" is a blasphemous expression. And it fitly describes the state of things in India, the mother, as I believe her to be, of Religion or religions. If she is truly the mother, the motherhood is on trial. Why should a Christian want to convert a Hindu to Christianity and vice versa? Why should he not be satisfied if the Hindu is a good or godly man! If the morals of a man are a matter of no concern, the form of worship in a particular manner is a church, a mosque or a temple is an empty formula; it may even be a hindrance to individual or social growth, and insistence on a particular form or repetition of a credo may be a potent cause of violent quarrels leading to bloodshed and ending in utter disbelief in Religion, i.e. God Himself.'

10. He goes on to say: 'Now one of the most intriguing texts on the universal and the particular that I know of in my beloved Bible is the passage in First Corinthians 15. (This is just an attempt to help those who love the Bible to think about these things, although others are allowed to listen in!) Let me tell it in the form of a Jewish-style midrash.

It is the day of consummation and the whole world is gathered and there we are, we Christians. Now as we look up there is God and Christ on God's right hand exactly as we have been told. So we turn around and see that there are also all the others. We see a sort of pan-religious and ecumenical representation and we turn around with a Christian smile which says: 'You see, it is just as we said and isn't it wonderful that our God is so generous that you can all be here!' When we turn back towards God there is no Christ to be seen on God's right side because Christ will never be present to feed into the smugness of his believers; or, as the text says: "And so when the end comes, Christ will lay it all down before the Father and God will become *panta en pasin,* all in all." That is another way of witnessing to the mystery—lest I be conceited.' Krister Stendahl, 'From God's Perspective we are all Minorities', *The Journal of Religious Pluralism* II:12 (1992).

11. Ibid.

12. Gandhi, *Hindu Dharma,* pp. 338–9. He goes on to say: 'The four varnas have been compared in the Vedas to the four members of the body, and no simile could be happier. If they are members of one body, how can one be superior or inferior to another? If the members of the body had the power of expression and each of them were to say that it was higher and better than the rest, the body would go to pieces. Even so, our body politic, the body of humanity, would go to pieces, if it were to perpetuate the canker of superiority or inferiority. It is this canker that is at the root of the various ills of our time, especially class-wars and civil strife. It should not be difficult for even the meanest understanding to see that these wars and strifes could not be ended except by the observance of the law of *varna.* For it ordains that every one shall fulfil the law of one's being by doing in a spirit of duty and service that to which one is born.'

13. Ibid., p. 324.

14. Mahadevan, *Outlines of Hinduism,* pp. 12–13.

15. P.V. Kane, *History of Dharmaśāstra* (Poona: Bhandarkar Oriental Research Institute, 1962), vol. V, pt. II, p. 1629.

16. Ibid., p. 1630.

17. G. Bühler, tr., *The Laws of Manu* (Delhi: Motilal Banarsidass, rpt. 1967, first published 1886), p. 30.

18. Gandhi, *Hindu Dharma,* p. 173.

19. Ibid., p. 11.

20. Ibid., p. 384.

21. Robert Payne, *The Life and Death of Mahatma Gandhi* (New York: E.P. Dutton and Co., 1969), p. 34.

22. Allama Muhammad Iqbal, *The Reconstruction of Religious Thought in Islam* (Lahore: Iqbal Academy Pakistan and Institute of Islamic Culture, 1989), pp. 100–1.

23. Shrimat Anirvan, 'Vedic Exegesis', in Haridas Bhattacharyya, ed., *The Cultural Heritage of India* (Calcutta: The Ramakrishna Mission Institute of Culture, 1958), vol. I, p. 323.

24. Mahadevan, *Outlines of Hinduism*, p. 40, n. 1.

25. See Hartmut Scharfe, *The State in Indian Tradition* (Leiden: E.J. Brill, 1989), p. 220, n. 125.

26. Ibid.

27. Kane, *History of Dharmaśāstra*, vol. V, pt. II, p. 1458.

28. Kisari Mohan Ganguli, tr., *The Mahabharata* (New Delhi: Munshiram Manoharlal, 1981: fourth edition), vol. III, pt. II, p. 604.

29. Ibid., p. 605.

30. Ibid., p. 610.

31. Jawaharlal Nehru, *The Discovery of India* (Calcutta: The Signet Press, 1946), p. 311.

32. See D.G. Tendulkar, *Mahatma: Life of Mohandas Karamchand Gandhi* (Government of India: The Publications Division, 1963), vol. VIII, p. 288.

33. Benjamin Walker, *The Hindu World* (New York: Frederick A. Praeger, 1968), vol. I, p. 325.

34. Bühler, *Laws of Manu*, p. 508.

35. Stuart W. Smithers, 'Spiritual Guide' in Mircea Eliade, Editor in Chief, *The Encyclopedia of Religion* (New York: Macmillan Publishing Company, 1987), vol. 14, p. 34.

36. Walker, *Hindu World*, vol. I, pp. 504–5.

37. See John Braisted Carman, *The Theology of Rāmānuja: An Essay in Interreligious Understanding* (New Haven and London: Yale University Press, 1974), pp. 39–41:

> The story of Rāmānuja's instruction from Tirukoṭṭiyūr Nambi (Goṣṭhī Pūrṇa) is one of the favourite parts of the biography and one very often

referred to in modern times in order to demonstrate Rāmānuja's liberal spirit. Rāmānuja went eighteen times from Srīrangam to the home of this disciple of Yāmuna in Tirukoṭṭiyūr. Each time Rāmānuja was sent off without being given the secret doctrine. Finally one of Nambi's disciples interceded. After adjuring Rāmānuja and his two inseparable disciples (Kūraṭṭālvān and Mudali Āṇḍān) to secrecy, Tirukoṭṭiyūr Nambi revealed the secret meaning of the eight-syllabled mantra, 'Oṁ Namo Nārāyaṇāya'. The very next day, however, Rāmānuja went up to the second-floor balcony of the temple tower in Tirukoṭṭiyūr and revealed the secret doctrine to a number of Śrī Vaiṣṇavas congregated in front of the main shrine below. (At the present time, this story is often told as though Rāmānuja had climbed to the *gopuram,* which is the tower over the gate of the temple, and had shouted the secret for all the townspeople to hear. In most temples the gopuram is indeed the only tower that one is permitted to climb. It would be disrespectful to climb up to the top of the *vimāna*, the tower above the central shrine, because one would then be higher than the Deity installed in the image below. In this particular temple, however, there is an image of the Deity on each of the three stories of the vimāna. The image at the top level shows the Deity in standing position, the image on the middle level in sitting position, and the one at ground level in recumbent position. Worshippers are permitted at all three levels. The earliest account makes clear that 'Rāmānuja revealed the meaning of the supreme secret to a number of Śrī Vaiṣṇavas'. Presumably they had all been duly initiated, but they may not have all been Brahmins. In any case, Tirukoṭṭiyūr Nambi had made Rāmānuja promise not to reveal the secret to anyone else.)

When Nambi heard what had happened, he was amazed and summoned Rāmānuja for an explanation. The ensuing conversation is reported as follows:

Nambi: I heard that you revealed this to a number of Śrī Vaiṣṇavas.

Uḍayavar: [*Rāmānuja*]. That is true. Taking your feet (committing myself to your mercy), I revealed it.

Nambi: Do you know the result of disobeying my command, when I told you not to tell anyone?

Uḍayavar: Going against the commandment of the ācārya will result in hell [naraka].

Nambi: Even knowing this, why have you told it?

Uḍayavar: I alone shall go to hell. Keeping your feet in mind I have revealed it. Thus because of their connection with you these souls will be saved.

Nambi then reflected, 'I am unable to attain this fullness.' Very much pleased with Rāmānuja's thought for the welfare of others, he called him to draw near and embraced him, calling him 'Emberumānār' (Our Lord), and said, 'What a great person you are. Up to this time this darśana was called *paramavaidika-darśanam*. From now on call it *Emberumānār darśanam*.'

The memory of the original event has been affected by a hundred years of recounting a favourite story, in which the secretiveness of Tirukoṭṭiyūr Nambi is vividly contrasted with Rāmānuja's open-hearted generosity: his desire to share the saving truth with others, not with all but certainly with all those who met the qualifications for such instruction. With each of Yāmuna's disciples, Rāmānuja began as an obedient disciple but then proceeded to demonstrate his own special gifts and finally his unique authority. One interesting feature of Rāmānuja's relation with these five mediators of Yāmuna's teaching is that each of the five is said to have committed one or more sons to Rāmānuja's care, henceforth to be his disciples.

It does not seem to me inconceivable that the incident at the Tirukoṭṭiyūr temple could have taken place, revolutionary as Rāmānuja's action would have been. Whatever happened, the story clearly captures a concern of Rāmānuja's that was to fill the rest of his life: to spread this darśana, which until now had been the carefully guarded property of a small group of devotees, to spread it both to the communities of devotees at other Vaiṣṇava temples and to the all-Indian scholarly community of students of the Sanskrit Scriptures.

38. Bimal Krishna Matilal, 'Kṛṣṇa: In Defence of a Devious Divinity', in Arvind Sharma, ed., *Essays on the Mahābhārata* (Leiden: E.J. Brill, 1991), p. 417.

39. Gandhi, *Hindu Dharma*, p. 279.

40. Ibid., p. 339.

41. Ibid., p. 330.

42. Ibid., p. 333.

43. Ibid., p. 345.

44. Ganguli, *Mahabharata*, vol. III, pt. II, p. 611.

45. Gandhi, *Hindu Dharma*, p. 3.

46. On how this option emerges from or at least relates to the previous ones, see Kane, *History of Dharmaśāstra*, vol. V, pt. II, pp. 1264–72.

47. Ibid., p. 1271.

48. Ibid., p. 1270.

49. Ibid., p. 1270.

50. S. Radhakrishnan, tr. and ed., *The Principal Upaniṣads* (London: George Allen & Unwin, 1953), p. 539.

51. Kane, *History of Dharmaśāstra*, vol. V, pt. II, p. 921, n. 1468(a); p. 924, n. 1476; p. 1642.

52. J.L. Shastri, *Manusmṛtiḥ* (Delhi: Motilal Banarsidass, 1983), p. 24.

53. Gandhi, *Hindu Dharma*, pp. 9, 339, 343.

54. Kane, *History of Dharmaśāstra*, vol. IV, pp. 926–67.

55. Ibid., vol. V, pt. II, pp. 1267–9.

56. D.H.J. Morgan, 'Sociology of Religion', in S.G.F. Brandon, *A Dictionary of Comparative Religion* (New York: Macmillan Publishing Company, 1970), p. 585.

57. Cited in Ibid.

Chapter 2
Karma and Rebirth Today

1. 'Whom Should I Mourn?', *Darshan* 14 (May 1988) p. 59.

2. Vettam Mani, *Puraṇic Encyclopedia* (Delhi: Motilal Banarsidass, 1975), p. 40 provides a slightly misleading account of this incident.

3. W. Norman Brown, *Man in the Universe: Some Continuities in Indian Thought* (Berkeley and Los Angeles: University of California Press, 1966), p. 82.

4. Philip H. Ashby, *Modern Trends in ·Hinduism* (New York and London: Columbia University Press, 1974), p. 64.

5. Ibid.

6. Bühler, *The Laws of Manu*, p. 61.

7. Mahadevan, *Outlines of Hinduism*, pp. 61–2.

8. M. Hiriyanna, *The Essentials of Indian Philosophy* (London: George Allen & Unwin, 1948), p. 55.

9. Louis Renou, ed., *Hinduism* (New York: George Braziller, 1962), pp. 55–6.

10. Ishwar C. Harris, *Radhakrishnan: The Profile of a Universalist* (Calcutta: Minerva Associates [Publications] Pvt. Ltd., 1982) p. 12.

11. Mahadevan, *Outlines of Hinduism*, p. vii.

12. Ibid., pp. vii–viii, emphasis added.

13. Kane, *History of Dharmaśāstra* vol. V, pt. II, pp. iv–vi.

Ethical standards are the only criteria for the distinction between high and low among men. Purity of conduct elevates a man even as impurity degrades him. All other distinctions are irrelevant. The *Chāndogya Upaniṣad* refers to *patitas*. The *Cāṇḍālas* are those given to stealing, drinking, adultery and murder. These four are fallen: *ete patanti catvāraḥ*. A patita, a fallen man, is a wicked man, a small-minded selfish man, not an untouchable.

The caste distinctions may have had their value in another context of society but we have out-grown it. The *Bhagavadgītā* speaks of the four-fold classification as based on guṇa (character) and karma (work).

We are all unregenerate at birth and become regenerate by our effort.

> *janmanā jāyate śūdraḥ*
> *saṁskārād dvija ucyate*

Some are advanced; others not. We should give equal facilities to all. The *Mahābhārata* says that there was only one varṇa at the beginning and the four castes arose out of later developments.

> *ekavarṇam idaṁ pūrvaṁ viśam āsīd yudhiṣṭhira*
> *karma-kriyā-vibhedena cāturvarṇyaṁ pratiṣṭhitam*

But we have come to base caste on birth though some of our leading writers have held that it is not birth or learning but conduct alone that constitutes its basis; for *dvijatva*,

> *vṛttam eva tu kāraṇam*
> *vedapāṭhena vipras tu brahmajñānāt tu brāhmaṇaḥ*

It is not the colour of the skin but the conduct of the person that counts. The only way to progress is by means of good conduct. The *Saṁvarta-Smṛti* says

> *sadācāreṇa devatvam ṛṣitvam vai tathaiva ca*
> *prāpnuvanti kuyonitvam manuṣyās tadviparyaye*

Great achievement is possible for each one of us.

Professor Kane brings out with great learning and lucidity the frequent changes our society has passed through. When Manu (I.85) tells us that different customs prevailed in different ages he suggests that the social code is not a fixed but a flexible one. Social customs and institutions are subject to change. Yājñavalkya tells us that 'one should not practise that which, though ordained by the *Smṛti*, is condemned by the people.' What appeals to one's conscience, *ātmanas tuṣṭiḥ*, the conscience of the disciplined, not of the superficial, the forms which the elect praise, should be our standard.

Vital changes may be introduced in the habits of the people by *pariṣads* or assemblies of the learned. When such assemblies cannot be constituted even the decision of one learned in dharma will be authoritative. The *Apastamba Dharmasūtra* says: *dharmajña-samayaḥ pramāṇam*. People who are learned and compassionate, who are practical-minded can decide the issues of right and wrong. They are the conscience of the community. What we are doing by legislative enactments is consistent with our tradition.

Chapter 3
Caste and the Stages of Life in Modern Living

1. Ainslie T. Embree, ed., *Alberuni's India* (New York: W.W. Norton and Company, Inc., 1971), pt. I, p. 100.

2. Ibid., p. 50.

3. '*Varna* is not caste, it is class. A man may call himself a *Brahmana*, i.e. a teacher of religion if he is one; or a *kshatriya*, a soldier if he is one; or a *vaishya*, i.e. a merchant or farmer if he is that; or a *shudra*, i.e. an employee if he is one. These divisions are not castes but classes and have reference to callings' (Gandhi, *Hindu Dharma*, pp. 312–13). Such a view involves an individualistic rather than a communal understanding of caste.

4. See Radhakrishnan, *The Hindu View of Life*, p. 85.

5. Khushwant Singh, *A History of the Sikhs* (Princeton, New Jersey: Princeton University Press, 1963), pp. 82–6.

6. Gandhi, *Hindu Dharma*, pp. 9, 343, etc.

7. Radhakrishnan, *The Hindu View of Life*, p. 87.

8. Ibid., p. 85.

9. Ibid.

10. P. V. Kane expresses a somewhat similar sentiment when he says: (see *History of Dharmaśāstra*, vol. V, pt. II, p. 1640): '… a generalisation was made that birth in a particular group or family was more or less sure indication of the possession of certain qualities generally associated with the members of that group or family'.

11. I owe the idea of associating political empowerment with *kṣatriyatva* to Professor T.N. Madan.

12. Kane, *History of Dharmaśāstra*, vol. II, pt. I, p. 423.

13. J. Duncan M. Derrett, *Religion, Law and the State in India* (New York: The Free Press, 1968), p. 108.

14. My reason for preferring renegotiation of the varṇa and the āśrama systems to their outright elimination has other reasons as well—although they are biographical rather than logical, unless one concedes that biography has a logic of his

own, just as we are told that the 'heart has its reasons which reason does not know of'. In the early 1980s, when I was teaching at the University of Sydney in Sydney, Australia, I was awarded a grant to carry out research on the caste system among the Hindus in the Fiji Islands, who were the descendants of indentured labourers. I was led to the project by the academic rumours I had heard, that the caste system had disappeared among the Hindus of Fiji. During the course of my research I discovered that such indeed was the case—in the sense that the Hindus interdined and intermarried freely across caste lines. In fact even my academic project was not considered above suspicion and a letter I received actually cast aspersions on my motives, as if I was an agent provocateur who had been sent to sow the seeds of dissension among the Hindus and stir up trouble by raising questions of caste. That was the one time in my life I have felt rather pleased by a false accusation, for it demonstrated that the Hindus of Fiji did consider themselves as a single religious community and would rather keep things that way. Thus the reports I had heard stood confirmed—and yet a great surprise lay in store for me. My field-notes consisted of two parts. In the first part I asked the respondents about what they regarded as the defining feature of Hinduism and in the second I drew their family tree, so to say, in terms of the caste affiliations of the various marriages which had made the tree grow. The surprise lay in the fact that almost everyone defined Hinduism—the Hinduism to which he or she subscribed—as varṇāśrama dharma and then proceeded to describe a family tree which had grafts on it from virtually every other tree in the garden!

It was then that I began giving more attention to the question of the ideological reorientation of the caste system itself—to the need to overcome this discrepancy between theory and practice. In this case praxis was guiding theory; the tail was wagging the dog but I felt a sense of discomfort at the prevailing state of affairs. It has been pointed out that our usual understanding of consistency involves the consistency of one *thought* with another, while the Gandhian concept of consistency involves the consistency of *thought* with *action*. In that sense I may be said to subscribe to the Gandhian tradition. Perhaps my uneasiness sprang from the fact that I did not fancy the traditional *concept* of caste lying embedded like a dormant virus or a recessive gene, in the body of Hinduism, and some genetic engineering seemed to be called for.

15. M. Hiriyanna, *The Essentials of Indian Philosophy* (London: George Allen & Unwin, 1949), p. 129, emphasis added. He goes on to say: 'Dr Randle ascribes this feature of the orthodox schools of thought to the circumstances that they had to face in Buddhism "a vigorous opposition which pressed free enquiry to the extreme limits of scepticism" and that it had be to met with its own weapons, which were perception and inference. The fortunate result of this,' he adds, 'was that the trammels of authority did not prevent the orthodox thinker from following where the argument leads.'

16. Embree, ed., *Alberuni's India*, vol. II, pp. 145–6. See also vol. I, pp. 396–7.

17. Ibid., p. 396.

18. Deborah A. Soifer, *The Myths of Narasiṁha and Vāmana: Two Avatars in Cosmological Perspective* (Albany: State University of New York Press, 1991).

19. Embree, *Alberuni's India*, p. 192.

20. Clifford Hospital, *The Righteous Demon: A Study of Bali* (Vancouver: University of British Columbia Press, 1984), p. 21.

21. Ibid., p. 218.

22. *Hinduism Today* 14, no. 12 (December 1992), p. 26.

23. A.S. Altekar, *The Position of Women in Hindu Civilization: From Prehistoric Times to the Present Day* (Delhi: Motilal Banarsidass, 1956) p. 68, n. 2.

24. Kane, *History of Dharmaśāstra*, vol. II, pt. I, p. 424.

25. Ibid., p. 426: 'Commentators like Sarvajña-Nārāyaṇa on Manu VI. 35 endeavour to bring about reconciliation between the three views set out above as follows: the view that a man may pass on to *saṁnyāsa* immediately after the period of student-hood (without being a householder) applies only to those men who are, owing to the impressions and effects of restrained conduct in past lives, entirely free from desires and whose tongue, sexual appetites, belly and words are thoroughly under control; the prescriptions of Manu enjoining on men not to resort to saṁnyāsa without paying off the three debts are concerned with men whose appetites have not yet thoroughly been brought under control and the words of Gautama that there is only one *āśrama* (that of the house-holder) relate only to those whose appetites for worldly pleasures and pursuits are quite keen.'

26. Monier Monier-Williams, *A Sanskrit-English Dictionary* (Oxford: Clarendon Press, 1964), p. 17, where it is translated as: 'superior to the four āśramas', an ascetic of the highest order'.

27. Radhakrishnan, *The Principal Upaniṣads*, p. 731: *ya eko'varṇo bahudhā śaktiyogād, varṇān anekān nihitārtho dadhāti* . . .

28. M. Hiriyanna, *Outlines of Indian Philosophy* (London: Allen & Unwin, 1948), p. 119, n. 2.

29. Shastry G.S. Sadhale, ed., *The Bhagavadgītā with Eleven Commentaries* (Bombay: The 'Gujarati' Printing Press, 1935), pp. 352–5.

Chapter 4
Hindu Tolerance

1. J.A. Dubois, *Hindu Manners, Customs, and Ceremonies*, ed. and tr. Henry K. Beauchamp (Oxford: Clarendon University Press, 1959), p. 119.

2. *The Complete Works of Swami Vivekananda*, vol. I, p. 4.

3. Nalini Devdas, *Swāmi Vivekānanda* (Bangalore: The Christian Institute for the Study of Religion and Society, 1968), p. 217; Walter G. Neevel, Jr., 'The Transformation of Sri Ramakrishna' in Bardwell L. Smith, ed., *Hinduism: New Essays in the History of Religions* (Leiden: E.J. Brill, 1976), p. 76.

4. Ainslie T. Embree, ed., *The Hindu Tradition: Readings in Oriental Thought* (New York: Random House, 1972), p. 303.

5. *The Life of Swami Vivekananda* by His Eastern and Western Disciples (Calcutta: Advaita Ashrama, 1965), p. 407.

6. Sailendra Nath Dhar, *A Comprehensive Biography of Swami Vivekananda* (Madras: Vivekananda Prakashan Kendra, 1975), pt. I, p. 464.

7. Ibid., p. 465.

8. Ibid., vol. I, p. 681.

9. *The Life of Swami Vivekananda*, p. 402.

10. Ibid., p. 404.

11. Ibid., p. 410.

12. Swami Nikhilananda, *Vivekananda: A Biography* (New York: Ramakrishna-Vivekananda Center, 1953), p. 114.

13. *The Life of Swami Vivekananda*, p. 374, emphasis added.

14. 'A recent Indologist in America claims to have compiled a list of over five thousand published works on this subject' (J.H. Hutton, *Caste in India* [Oxford University Press, 1961], p. xiii).

15. See R.C. Zaehner, *Hinduism* (Oxford University Press, 1962), p. 4; also see chapter seven.

16. Ibid., p. 198.

17. Ibid., pp. 220–3.

18. See Manusmṛti X.4; see Bühler, *Laws of Manu* (Oxford: Clarendon Press, 1886), p. 402.

19. Manusmṛti X.74–80; see Bühler, *Laws of Manu*, pp. 419–20; also see Manusmṛti XI.81–117.

20. See Manusmṛti X; Bühler, *Laws of Manu*, pp. 401–30.

21. 'Every Hindu is in traditional theory born to a caste, in which he must remain for life, and he is bound to live by its rules, subject to severe consequences for failure. A caste is a hereditary endogamous group, which has a name of its own

and some special traits of occupation, cult, or custom, giving it a separate place in the system. A man must take his wife from his caste—there are a few well-defined exceptions—usually can eat only with caste fellows and is ranked in the social scale by the nature of the traditional customs of his caste. No individual can in accepted theory become a Hindu and enter a caste, though under certain conditions a group may. Hence Hinduism is a non-proselytizing faith' (W. Norman Brown, *The United States and India and Pakistan* [Harvard University Press, 1963], p. 33). It is helpful, at this point, to distinguish between two issues: (1) conversion to Hinduism in particular; (2) and conversion in general from any one religion to another. W. Norman Brown's statement explains why there may be no conversion to Hinduism. In the next section an attempt is made to explain how the same theoretical system also suggests a doctrine of non-conversion from any one religion to another, again using the illustrative case of the possibility of conversion to Hinduism. It will be noticed that as one moves from (1) to (2) the key category shifts from that of caste to its logically antecedent—that of Karma.

22. See Mahadevan, *Outlines of Hinduism*, p. 295.

23. If it be argued that the Swāmī did allow room for change when he said that if after trying first to be a true Christian, 'even then you feel unfulfilled, it will be time to consider what should be done' (ibid.), then it may be pointed out that even in the classical scheme of varṇa it was possible to change one's occupation (see Manusmṛti X.81–117) and even one's varṇa (see Manusmṛti VII.42 for example) in exceptional circumstances.

24. It must be pointed out, however, that this presentation has several limitations, though the point it makes within these limitations may appear to possess a certain appeal. (1) There is more than one attitude towards the varṇa schema in Hinduism (see J. Muir, *Original Sanskrit Texts*, [Amsterdam: Oriental Press, 1967], pp. 159–60; K.M. Sen, *Hinduism*, [Baltimore: Penguin Books, 1973], pp. 27–31) and more than one attitude towards conversion as well (see Edward C. Dimock Jr., 'Doctrine and Practice among the Vaiṣṇavas of Bengal', *History of Religions* [1963], vol. 3, no. 1, p. 122). (2) The doctrines of karma and rebirth are shared by Buddhism and Hinduism but in the case of Buddhism it 'is significant that it was able to combine a missionary zeal with this tolerant outlook' (K.N. Jayatilleke, *The Buddhist Attitude to Other Religions* [Ceylon: Public Trustee Department, 1966], p. 1). But again, significantly, Buddhism did not approve of the *rigidity* of the caste system in particular and tended to question it in general. (3) Some historians have argued that a *flexible* caste system may have facilitated the expansion of Hinduism all over India (see Ram Sharan Sharma, *Śūdras in Ancient India* [(Delhi: Motilal Banarsidass, 1958], p. 29 and chapter II) so that conversion and the caste system can also be positively connected in some historical situations.

25. Klaus K. Klostermaier, *A Survey of Hinduism* (Albany, New York: State University of New York Press, 1989), p. 59.

26. Kane, *History of Dharmaśāstra*, vol. v, pt. II, p. 1624.

27. S. Radhakrishnan, *The Bhagavadgītā* (London: George Allen & Unwin, 1948), p. 159.

28. Kane, *History of Dharmaśāstra*, vol. v, pt. II, p. 1624.

29. Radhakrishnan, *The Bhagavadgītā*, p. 159.

30. Ibid., p. 159, n. 5.

31. K. Satchidananda Murty, *Vedic Hermeneutics* (Delhi: Motilal Banarsidass, 1993), p. xii.

32. S. Radhakrishnan, tr., *The Brahma Sūtra: The Philosophy of Spiritual Life* (London: George Allen & Unwin, 1960), pp. 162–3.

33. Arvind Sharma, 'Some Misunderstandings of the Hindu Approach to Religious Plurality', *Religion* (8), pp. 143–5.

34. Anonymous remarks of a reader.

35. Keshavram Narasimha Iengar, 'Varnasrama Vyavastha', in *Dilip* 20(3) (July/September 1994), p. 28, n. 17.

36. Heinrich Zimmer, *Myths and Symbols in Indian Art and Civilization*, ed. Joseph Campbell (New York and Evanston: Harper & Row, 1946), p. 181.

Chapter 5
Hinduism and the Future

1. Renou, *Hinduism*, pp. 56–7.

2. Gandhi, *Hindu Dharma*, p. 237.

3. Cited by Donald Eugene Smith, *India as a Secular State* (Princeton, New Jersey: Princeton University Press, 1963), pp. 348–9.

4. Ibid.

5. Mahadevan, *Outlines of Hinduism*, p. 283.

6. Smith, *India as a Secular State*, p. 351.

7. Ibid., p. 354, emphasis added.

8. Ibid., pp. 498–9, emphasis added:

'What is the meaning of the term "secular state" in the Indian context? This might at first appear to be a point of academic significance only, but its practical implications are immediate and profound. The most basic question is simply whether the secular state means (1) a state which aids all religions impartially, or (2) a state which is separate from religion. If it is the latter, then the ideal will be for the state to aid no religion, to assume no religious functions.

This is an old and familiar problem in the United States, and the Supreme Court still vacillates between the "no-preference" doctrine and the "wall of separation" doctrine. The tax exemption granted to all religious institutions illustrates the first doctrine; the absolute prohibition of the appropriation of public funds to support religious institutions illustrates the second. The Constitution of India prohibits only special taxes for the support of "any particular religion" but would presumably permit a general tax for the support of all religions. This expression of the "no-preference" doctrine must be contrasted with the "wall of separation" prohibition of all forms of religious instruction in state schools.

In India there is a strong inclination to support the "no-preference" doctrine. It is in keeping with some of the traditions of the Hindu state and is closely allied to the neo-Hindu emphasis that all religions are true. *There is a real danger that the "no-preference" doctrine may be used to justify state promotion of a syncretistic "Universal Religion of Man" which is nevertheless based on Hindu assumptions. This tendency was clearly revealed in the Radhakrishnan report on university education.*'

9. To the objections raised by Western scholars in the context of the promotion of the study of all the world's religions, I would like to share my experience of editing the book called *Our Religions.* Consider the title 'Our Religions'. It is an expression used by Mahatma Gandhi and is pregnant with meaning. The Executive Editor of Harper San Francisco once remarked: 'In the present-day world, although we nominally belong to one particular tradition, functionally we draw upon all—albeit at times unconsciously'. I thought he captured the existential situation of many of us rather well when he said that—that we are nominally singular but functionally plural. This attitude bears the imprimatur of approval from no less a figure than Gandhi who defined his Hinduism as including the *best* of all religions, which resonates with Matthew Arnold's famous definition of culture as consisting of the *best* that has been thought and said in the world. If, however, we add to this the comment that in seeking perfection the best is only good enough, then room is created for what I wish to say next.

As I reflect on that statement a new element, almost painful but probably also salutary, creeps into my reflections. All the religions of the world are great, but are they perfect? We prefer to speak of truth but what about error? For sure, I share the Hindu epistemological optimism that if error comes can truth be far behind. But what if truth does not always bring up the rear? We all know that Hinduism—justly or unjustly—has been associated, at least in the popular imagination and not only in the popular imagination, with inegalitarianism; Islam with violence, Christianity with Imperialism and the roll call can go on. It could, of course, be asserted that perhaps a present limitation of a tradition has been misconstrued as an inherent limitation in one case as I have repeatedly pointed out, or that what is specific to a tradition has been confused with what is essential in another; and that elsewhere what is pathological has been mistaken for what is normal. Elegant explanations are possible, offered by people of will and goodwill, whose motives are untainted by apologetics, and who often don't even belong to the faith they happen to be defending. When we add to this the fact that what the critics have considered loopholes have sometimes become leapholes through which a religious tradition has gained a spiritual footing at a higher level, we may tend to be less severe in our judgment. However, in the context of the present book and the present discussion I would like to propose another perspective. If truth presupposes the possibility of error and it is conceded that in some respects, at some time, somehow, some of the religions may have at least fallen into error, even if error does not belong to them, then the question arises: To whom does that error belong? If the religions are *our* religions, then is not their error but *our* error? Are we just going to be fair-weather friends of our religions, take what we like best from them and forsake them in their hour of need? I must confess that when I first turned my imagination in this direction strange feelings arose in my heart for which as yet I have no words. This is a case not of a mystical but rather an introspective lack of articulation, for I could no longer look upon the alleged shortcomings of religions other than my own, as other than my own! I could still criticise them but such criticism now became self-criticism; I could still accuse them but such accusations became self-reproach. What I mean to say is: If I belong to all religions I have no fifth amendment left to protect me against self-incrimination. For if all religions are ours then only by taking responsibility for their shortcomings can we participate in their greatness. I envision Hinduism's fellowship with the religions of the world in this spirit.

10. I owe this felicitous formulation to Professor Thomas Berry of Fordham University.

Index